INTERACTIONS II
A Listening/Speaking Skills Book

INTERACTIONS II
A Listening/Speaking Skills Book

Judith Tanka
University of California at Los Angeles

Lida R. Baker
University of California at Los Angeles

RANDOM HOUSE   New York

This book was developed for Random House by Eirik Børve, Inc.

To Our Parents

First Edition

9 8 7 6 5 4 3 2 1

Library of Congress Cataloging in Publication Data

Tanka, Judith, 1950–
      Interactions 2. A listening/speaking book.

      1. English language—Text-books for foreign speakers.
2. Listening.   3. Oral communication.   I. Baker, Lida R.
II. Title.
PE1128.T3252   1985   428.3'4   85-2046
ISBN 0-394-33708-5

Manufactured in the United States of America

Text design and production: Donna Davis
Cover design: Cheryl Carrington
Cover photo: Peter Menzel
Drawings: Sally Richardson
Photo research: Lindsay Kefauver

Photo Credits
Page 29, left, reprinted with permission of Federal Express Corporation. All rights reserved; right, courtesy of Apple Computer, Inc.; p. 35, Mike Mazzaschi/Stock, Boston; p. 40, left, Olof Källström/Jeroboam, Inc.; right, Bohdan Hrynewych/Stock, Boston; p. 41, left, Donald Dietz/Stock, Boston; right, Peter Menzel/Stock, Boston; p. 50, Elizabeth Hamlin/Stock, Boston; p. 73, left, Gregg Mancuso/Stock, Boston; right, James A. Sugar/Black Star; p. 75, left, Peter Menzel/Stock, Boston; right, Owen Franken/Stock, Boston; p. 86, left, Wayne Miller/Magnum Photos Inc.; right, Burt Glinn/Magnum Photos Inc.; p. 87, Fredrik D. Bodin/Stock, Boston; p. 97, NASA; p. 121, Donald Dietz/Stock, Boston; p. 122, left, Kent Reno/Jeroboam, Inc.; right, Bruce Kliewe/Stock, Boston; p. 137, left, Eileen Christelow/Jeroboam, Inc.; right, AP/Wide World Photos.

CONTENTS

Chapter 12   PREJUDICE, TOLERANCE, AND JUSTICE   132

> *Subtopics:* discrimination (racial, religious, etc.), prayer in public
>   schools, minority groups
>
> *Reductions:* reduced forms of perfect modals
>
> *Functions:* speculating about past events

PREFACE

INTERACTIONS: THE PROGRAM

INTERACTIONS consists of eight texts plus two instructor's manuals for in-college or college-bound nonnative English students. INTERACTIONS I is for high-beginning to low-intermediate students, while INTERACTIONS II is for low-intermediate to intermediate students. Within each level, I and II, the books are carefully coordinated by theme, vocabulary, grammar structure, and, where possible, language functions. A chapter in one book corresponds to and reinforces material taught in the same chapter of the other three books at that level for a truly integrated, four-skills approach.

Each level, I and II, consists of four books plus an instructor's manual. In addition to *A Listening/Speaking Skills Book*, they include:

A Communicative Grammar I, II: Organized around grammatical topics, these books include notional/functional material where appropriate. They present all grammar in context and contain a wide variety of communicative activities.

A Reading Skills Book I, II: The selections in these books are written by the authors and carefully graded in level of difficulty and amount of vocabulary. They include many vocabulary-building exercises and emphasize reading strategies: for example, skimming, scanning, guessing meaning from context, understanding the structure and organization of a selection, increasing reading speed, and interpreting the author's point of view.

A Writing Process Book I, II: These books use a process approach to writing, including many exercises on prewriting and revision. Exercises build skills in exploring and organizing ideas, developing vocabulary, using correct form and mechanics, using coherent structure, editing, revising, and using feedback to create a final draft.

Instructor's Manual I, II: These manuals provide instructions and guidelines for use of the books separately or in any combination to form a program. For each of the core books, there is a separate section with teaching tips and other suggestions. The instructor's manuals also include sample tests.

The grammatical focus for the twelve chapters of INTERACTIONS II is as follows:

1 review of basic verb tenses
2 nouns, pronouns, adjectives, and articles
3 modal auxiliaries and related structures
4 the present perfect with *still, yet,* etc.; *would/used to, was/were going to;* the past perfect tense
5 phrasal verbs and related structures
6 coordinating conjunctions; clauses of time, condition, reason, contrast, and purpose; the future perfect tense
7 transitions; the past perfect continuous tense; clauses of time
8 clauses and phrases of comparison
9 the passive voice
10 adjective clauses
11 common uses of infinitives and gerunds
12 *wish, hope,* and imaginative conditional sentences

INTERACTIONS II: A LISTENING/SPEAKING SKILLS BOOK

When listening to English, lower-level students have two basic needs:

1. to understand the essence of messages beyond their level, i.e., day-to-day comprehension for survival
2. to learn effective listening strategies that, in turn, will lead to language acquisition itself

Whereas traditional emphasis in lower-level listening texts has typically been on testing comprehension, *Interactions II: A Listening/Speaking Skills Book* is concerned with teaching low-intermediate or intermediate students *how to listen.*

Chapter Organization

Organized around a theme, each chapter is divided into four listening strategies and a speaking section:

Part I   Getting the Main Idea; Stressed Words and Reductions

1. As students listen to an introductory conversation, they actively focus on the stressed words that signal important information.
2. Students learn to recognize and reproduce reduced forms common in spoken American English.

Part II   Lecture

Students listen to a lecture and take notes by filling in an incomplete outline. Based on their notes, students answer comprehension questions and define new vocabulary.

Part III   Making Inferences

Students use contextual clues to understand implied messages in a conversation. Since the answers to the questions appear later in the conversation itself, students get the benefit of immediate feedback.

Part IV   Listening Tasks

In this section students demonstrate their comprehension by performing practical tasks involving material such as drawings, maps, and application forms.

Part V   Speaking Activities

Role-plays, small-group activities, and class discussions complement the listening component. These speaking activities are natural extensions of the chapter theme and offer imaginative opportunities to further explore it.

Teaching Suggestions

The philosophy behind this book is to teach students listening skills that will help them distinguish the forest from the trees in their complex listening environment— i.e., the real world. Consequently, the exercises will seem quite challenging. While the exercises themselves aren't extremely complicated, they do depend heavily on the students' full understanding of the instructions and goals. Therefore, we recommend that teachers spend sufficient time clarifying the purpose and method of each exercise prior to assigning it.

For further specific teaching guidelines, consult the instructor's manual.

Ancillaries

1. Tape program and key, to be used in conjunction with the student book
2. Instructor's manual

ACKNOWLEDGMENTS

Of the many people who in various ways helped us complete this book, we would especially like to thank our colleagues at UCLA, Mary McVey Gill and the staff of Eirik Børve, Inc., and Mr. K.

INTERACTIONS II
A Listening/Speaking Skills Book

1
EDUCATION AND STUDENT LIFE

PART I. PHONOLOGICAL CLUES

Context: The following conversation between an American teacher and a foreign student takes place on a college campus. This is their first meeting.

   Preview questions: Where do you think they're going? Why are they there? Who will start the conversation? What time of year is it? Is there anything else you would like to know about them?

Getting the Main Idea

A. Listen to the conversation. Listen for the main ideas only.

B. Discuss your answers to the preview questions. Were your predictions correct? What else do you remember about Gloria and Linda?

Stress

C. In spoken English, important words—words that carry information—are usually stressed. This means they are:

a. higher pitched,

b. louder,

c. pronounced more clearly.

Listen to the conversation again and fill in the missing stressed words.

Gloria: _____ me. Could you _____ me

_____ Kimbel _____ is?

Linda: Oh, you mean _____ Hall?

Gloria: Yeah, _____ _____ .

Linda: It's _____ over _____ .

_____ going there, too. Are you _____

the _____ _____ test?

Gloria: Yes, I _____ . How about _____ ?

Linda: _____ one of the _____

_____ here.

Gloria: Oh, _____ ? _____ I'll be in your

_____ .

Linda: It's _____ . What's your _____ ?

Gloria: Gloria Santos.

Linda: _____ name is _____ . Are you from

_____ _____ ?

Gloria: _____ , I'm from _____ .

D. Now listen to the first part of the conversation again. Repeat each sentence after the speaker. Remember: stressed words are *louder and clearer* than unstressed words.

E. Listen to the rest of the conversation and write the important (stressed) words. Your notes should look like a telegram.

Linda: *been here long* _____

Gloria: _____

Linda: _____

Gloria: _____

Linda: _____

Gloria: _____

Linda: _____

Gloria: _____

Linda: _____

Gloria: _____

Linda: _____

_____

Gloria: _____

F. Using your notes, reconstruct the conversation with a partner, orally or in writing.

Reductions

G. In spoken English, words that are not stressed are often shortened or reduced. For example: "Could you tell me where Campbell Hall is?" changes to: "*Cudja tell me where Campbell Hall is?" Listen to the difference:

Long: could you

Short: *cudja

There are several examples of reduced forms in the conversation you just heard. Listen to these examples of long and short forms and repeat the *short form* after the speaker.

Oh, you mean Campbell Hall?

How about you?

I'm one of the English teachers here.

What's your name?

My family used to come here every summer.

Now I want to go to college here.

Will you have to take the TOEFL?

H. Listen to the reductions in the following conversation between a foreign student and a school secretary. Write the *long form* in the blanks.

A: _____ _____ help me? I _____

_____ be _____ _____

the students here. I _____ _____ get

an application for the TOEFL test.

B: _____ _____ the one in November?

Let's see. The applications _____ _____

be on this shelf. It looks like they're all gone. You'll probably

_____ _____ wait until next week.

A: _____ _____ sending me one when

they come in?

B: Sure. _____ _____ name and address?

An asterisk (*) tells you that the following word or words is a reduced form—not standard English.

PART II. LECTURE

Context: Gloria goes to an orientation meeting for foreign students. At the lecture, the speaker provides information about typical college or university courses in the United States and Canada.

Preview questions: What do you already know about college courses in this country? Think of areas such as exams, class size, student-teacher relationships, grades, etc.

Vocabulary: The following terms appear in the lecture. Try to understand them from the context they are in; do not use a dictionary. After the lecture, you will be asked to write a brief definition of each term.

lecture	midterm exam
discussion section	essay question
teaching assistant	research paper

A. Listen to the lecture. Follow the outline as you listen. Do not write anything at this point.

B. Listen again and fill in the outline.

OUTLINE
A Typical University Course

I. Introduction

II. Undergraduate course description

   A. Lectures

      1. Hours/week: _____

      2. Class size: _____

      3. Classes taught by professors

      4. Note-taking important

         a. _____

         b. _____

   B. _____

      1. Hours/week: _____

      2. Class size: _____

      3. Purpose: to ask questions

      4. Taught by _____

   C. Lab—especially for _____ majors

III. Exams

   A. Number of exams

      1. _____

      2. _____

   B. Types of written exams

      1. Objective

      2. _____

IV. _____

   A. Choose topic

   B. Go to library

   C. _____

   D. _____

V. If you need help

    A. Find out when instructor has office hours

    B. Make _____

C. Listen to the following questions and write the answers.

    1. If a student is taking three classes, about how many hours per week will he or she spend attending lectures? _____

    2. Why is it important to take notes during college lectures?

    _____

    _____

    3. What are two ways in which science and nonscience majors differ?

    _____

    _____

    4. What are two general categories of exam questions?

    _____

    5. What should you do if you are having trouble in class?

    _____

D. *Vocabulary review.* Define these terms as they were used in the lecture.

    1. lecture: _____

    _____

    2. discussion section: _____

    _____

    3. teaching assistant: _____

    _____

    4. midterm exam: _____

    _____

    5. essay question: _____

    _____

    6. research paper: _____

    _____

PART III. MAKING INFERENCES

The following short conversations take place on a college campus. After each conversation you will hear a question. Circle the correct answer. Then listen to the conversation again. This time you will hear the correct answer.

1. a. in a bookstore
   b. in a library
   c. in a laboratory

2. a. a secretary
   b. a teacher
   c. his roommate

3. a. chemistry
   b. history
   c. German

4. a. interested
   b. uninterested
   c. afraid

5. a. happy
   b. uninterested
   c. afraid

PART IV. LISTENING TASKS

A. Listen to the following telephone conversation between a foreign student and a college counselor. Complete the application form using the information in the conversation.

PLEASE PRINT CLEARLY (OR TYPE):

Name _____ Telephone number _____
      last (family name)   first   middle

Current mailing address _____
                   number and street   city   state   ZIP

Date of birth _____ Country of birth _____
         month/day/year

Country of citizenship _____

Type of visa _____

Expiration date _____

Referred by _____
      consulate, sponsoring agency, travel agency, friend, advertisement, former student, other

B. Look at the map of the college campus. Find Memorial Cafeteria. Linda is sitting outside the cafeteria when some students approach her to ask directions. Listen to the directions Linda gives. Then write the names of the buildings you hear on the map.

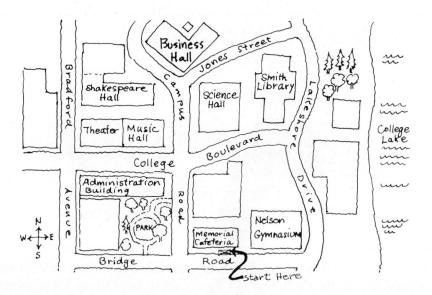

PART V. SPEAKING ACTIVITIES

A. *Discussion.* Compare the American university system with that of your country. Discuss the following areas:

- types of colleges (two-year, four-year, etc.)
- entrance requirements
- years of study
- grades
- class size
- types and frequency of exams
- degrees
- graduation requirements
- teacher-student relationships

B. *Role-play.* With a partner, act out the following situations.

1. You need to make an appointment with your instructor to discuss the course (tests, grades, etc.).

2. You were absent on the first day of your English class. Ask your teacher or a classmate about the course requirements.

3. Find out how to get from your classroom to the language laboratory (library, cafeteria) at your school.

4. Using Conversations 4 and 5 in Part III as models, act out conversations about accepting or refusing a date. Be sure to vary your intonation.

C. *Activities.*

1. Call the foreign student office in your school. Find out how many students from your country are enrolled at your school. Report the number to your class.

2. Go to the library. Look at a college or university catalogue other than your own school's. Find the requirements for your major and give a brief report to the class.

2
CITY LIFE

PART I. PHONOLOGICAL CLUES

Context: The following phone conversation is about an ad for a roommate to share a house. The speakers are the owner of the house and a student looking for a place to live.

Preview questions: What will the student want to know about the house? What will the owner want to know about the student?

Getting the Main Idea

A. Listen to the conversation. Listen for the main ideas only.

B. Discuss your answers to the preview questions. Were your predictions correct? What did you learn about Jeff and Gloria?

Stress

C. Listen to the conversation again and fill in the missing stressed words.

    Linda: Hello?

    Gloria: _____ I speak to Linda?

    Linda: Speaking.

    Gloria: Hi. My name is Gloria. I'm _____ about the

        _____ for rent.

    Linda: Oh, _____ . Are you a _____ ?

    Gloria: Well, _____ _____ I'm studying

        _____ , but I'm _____ to start

        _____ full _____ in March.

    Linda: Where are you living _____ ?

    Gloria: I've been _____ with some other

        _____ since _____ , but I don't

        _____ it there.

    Linda: What's the _____ ?

    Gloria: It's too _____ and I want more

        _____ .

    Linda: Well, it's _____ _____ . We're not

        _____ very much.

    Gloria: _____ do you _____ ?

    Linda: I'm an _____ teacher at the _____ .

D. Now listen to the first part of the conversation again. Repeat each sentence after the speaker. Remember: stressed words are *louder and clearer* than unstressed words.

E. Listen to the rest of the conversation and write the important (stressed) words. Your notes should look like a telegram.

    Gloria: _____

        _____

    Linda: _____

        _____

        _____

    Gloria: _____

Linda: _____

_____

_____

Gloria: _____

Linda: _____

Gloria: _____

Linda: _____

_____

Gloria: _____

Linda: _____

_____

Gloria: _____

Linda: _____

F. Using your notes, reconstruct the conversation with a partner, orally or in writing.

Reductions

G. Listen to these examples of long and short forms from the conversation and repeat the *short forms* after the speaker.

> Where are you living now?
> What do you do?
> How do you feel about a male roommate?
> You can walk from here.
> Can you make it this evening around five?
> See you then.

H. Now listen to the reductions in the following conversations. Write the *long forms* in the blanks.

G: Hey Jeff, _____ _____

_____ _____

_____ going?

J: I _____ _____ get a present for

Linda. It's her birthday, you know.

G: Yeah, I know. _____ _____

_____ think I should _____ _____

_____ ?

J: Well, she likes music. _____ _____ a

  record?

L: _____ _____ _____

  like my new haircut, Gloria?

G: It's great! _____ _____

  _____ hairdresser?

L: His name's José.

G: _____ _____ give me his phone

  number?

L: Sure, but he's always very busy. _____

  _____ try calling him, but he might not be able

  _____ _____ _____

  until next month.

J: _____ _____ _____

  make guacamole?

G: I'm not sure. I _____ _____

  _____ _____ cook Mexican food.

PART II. LECTURE

Context: In many American cities, people in some neighborhoods have gotten together and formed "Neighborhood Watches." This means that the neighbors agree to work together to prevent crime in their area. At the first Neighborhood Watch meeting, a policeman usually comes to speak to the neighbors.

Last week there was a burglary in Linda and Jeff's neighborhood. The people on their street decided to form a Neighborhood Watch. This is their first meeting. The policeman is speaking about ways to prevent burglary.

Preview questions: Have you ever heard of a Neighborhood Watch? Does your neighborhood have one? Can you think of some ways to protect your home against crime?

**GOOD
NEIGHBORS
PROTECT
EACH OTHER.**

**THROUGH...
NEIGHBORHOOD
WATCH**

Vocabulary: The following terms appear in the lecture. Try to understand them from the context they are in; do not use a dictionary. After the lecture, you will be asked to write a brief definition of each term.

to prevent	decal
burglar	timer
burglary	dead bolt
	valuables

A. Listen to the lecture. Follow the outline as you listen. Do not write anything at this point.

B. Listen again and fill in the outline.

OUTLINE
Burglary Prevention

I. Lights

  A. Outside

    1. _____

    2. _____

B. Inside

    1. Automatic timer

    2. In apartment building, check _____

II. Locks

    1. _____

    2. _____

III. _____

    1. Don't keep at home

    2. Mark them

IV. Neighborhood Watch

    1. When on vacation

       a. _____

       b. _____

    2. Unusual activities

    _____

    3. Put decal in window

C. Listen to the following questions and write the answers.

    1. Why is it important to turn on the lights in front and in the back of the house?

    _____

    _____

    2. What type of locks did the policeman recommend?

    _____

    3. How does an automatic timer work?

    _____

    4. Why should you mark your t.v., stereo, and other valuables?

    _____

    5. What should you do before you go on vacation?

    _____

    _____

D. *Vocabulary review.* Define these terms as they were used in the lecture.

1. to prevent: _____

_____

2. burglar: _____

_____

3. burglary: _____

_____

4. decal: _____

_____

5. timer: _____

_____

6. dead bolt: _____

_____

7. valuables: _____

_____

PART III. MAKING INFERENCES

Listen to the following conversations, which take place in an apartment building. After each conversation you will hear a question. Circle the correct answer. Then listen again. This time you will hear the correct answer.

1. a. the apartment manager
   b. a neighbor
   c. Mina's roommate

2. a. repairman
   b. a painter
   c. an exterminator

3. a. It's on the third floor.
   b. It's in bad condition.
   c. It's luxurious.

4. a. He doesn't mind at all.
   b. He's surprised to see Mina.
   c. He's a little angry.

5. a. He doesn't mind at all.
   b. He's surprised to see Mina.
   c. He's a little angry.

PART IV. LISTENING TASKS

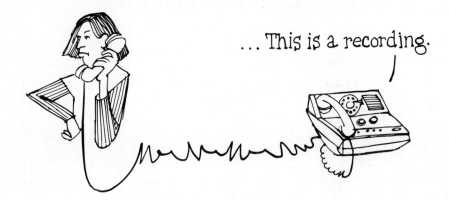

... This is a recording.

Have you ever called a place for help or information and gotten a recording? What was the place? What did the recording say? Many businesses use recordings to save time and money, especially after office hours. You are going to hear several recordings of this type. After each recording, fill in the missing information.

1. Place: _____

Business hours: times: _____ to _____

days: _____ to _____

Repair number: _____

2. Place: _____

Business hours: times: _____ to _____

days: _____ to _____

In emergency: _____

3. Place: _____

Hours: times: _____ to _____ days: _____

times: _____ to _____ days: _____

Bell Theater number: _____

For more information: _____

4. Place: _____

Travel and weather information: time: _____ to _____

days: _____

Emergency roadside service: _____

5. Place: _____

Hospital emergency service: _____

Emergency police service: _____

Hospital patient information: _____

Other hospital information: _____

PART V. SPEAKING ACTIVITIES

A. *Telephone practice.* Below is a list of commonly used services. Look in the yellow pages of your phone book and choose one company for each category.

Then divide into groups. Each person in the group calls one company from the list and asks for the indicated information. Later, each person reports to the class to compare who found the cheapest prices. Practice forming questions in your groups before you make your calls.

1. Service: moving truck rental

   Budget
   Ryder
   U-Haul

   Company name: _____ Phone: _____

   Situation: You are moving from an apartment to a home about five miles away. You need to rent a small truck to move your things.

   Suggested questions: size of truck you need   *Day available*
   cost per day   *Insurance*
   cost per week
   cost per mile
   pick-up and return points

2. Service: plumber

   Roto-rooter

   Company name: _____ Phone: _____

   Situation: Your toilet is backed up. You need a plumber as soon as possible.

   Suggested questions: cost per hour   *When*
   cost on weekday/weekend   *What should I do*
   cost after hours

3. Service: carpet cleaning

   Company name: _____ Phone: _____

   Situation: Your wall-to-wall carpeting (1100 sq. feet) needs to be cleaned.

   Suggested questions: free estimate   *when*
   cost

4. Service: pizza delivery

   Restaurant name: _____ Phone: _____

   Situation: You want a large pizza with sausage and olives delivered to your house.

   Suggested questions: price of pizza   *How quick*
   delivery charge

5. Service: dry cleaning

   Company name: _____ Phone: _____

   Situation: You have a man's white silk shirt with coffee stains.

   Suggested questions: cost
   extra charge for stain
   same day service

B. *Role-play.* Using the conversations in Part III as a model, act out a conversation about a tenant complaining to a manager. Choose one of the following problems and work out a solution for it.

1. leaky plumbing

2. insects

3. exposed wiring

4. broken garbage disposal

5. broken toilet

C. *Game.* Pretend that you have enough money to build the house of your dreams. Describe your dream house in detail. What kind of house will you build? What will it look like? What furniture will you choose?

Sit in a circle. One person says: "In my dream house I will have wall-to-wall carpeting." The next person *repeats* the first sentence and *adds* one item. The next person repeats both items and adds another, and so on.

Example: "In my dream house I will have wall-to-wall carpeting and a painting by Picasso."

You can stay in the game as long as you remember all the items. When you make a mistake, you're *out!*

3
BUSINESS AND MONEY

PART I. PHONOLOGICAL CLUES

Context: Gloria now lives with Linda and Jeff. In the following conversation, Jeff gives Gloria advice about investments.

Preview questions: What do people in your country invest in when they have extra money? What do you think Jeff will advise Gloria to do?

Getting the Main Idea

A. Listen to the conversation. Listen for the main ideas only.

B. Discuss your answers to the preview questions. Were your predictions correct? What three things did Jeff advise Gloria to do?

Stress

C. Listen to the conversation again and fill in the missing stressed words.

Gloria: I _____ this _____ . Do you

_____ it?

Jeff: Yeah. Linda and I inherited _____ when our

_____ died. We _____ thought of

investing in _____ things, like the

_____ market, but in the _____ ,

we _____ we'd _____ buy a

_____ together.

Gloria: Wasn't it _____ ?

Jeff: Well, we _____ it when you could _____

get something _____ in this neighborhood for a

reasonable _____ . _____ ,

you _____ ; the _____ are too

_____ . Of course, the _____ didn't

_____ like _____ when we

_____ it. We had to do a lot of _____

on it before we were _____ to _____

_____ . _____ was

_____ _____ ago.

Gloria: My _____ would like to _____ in

something here, but he's not _____ what the

_____ are. Since I'm a _____ major,

he _____ I ought to _____ some

_____ , so he's asked _____ to do

some _____ for him. Can you

_____ me any _____ ?

D. Now listen to the first part of the conversation again. Repeat each sentence after the speaker. Remember: stressed words are *louder and clearer* than unstressed words.

E. Listen to the rest of the conversation and write the important (stressed) words. Your notes should look like a telegram.

Jeff: _____

_____

_____

Gloria: _____

Jeff: _____

Gloria: _____

F. Using your notes, reconstruct the conversation with a partner, orally or in writing.

Reductions

G. Listen to these examples of long and short forms from the conversation and repeat the *short form* after the speaker.

Do you own it?
Linda and I inherited money.
You should call and ask.
We had to do a lot of work.
We were able to move in.
My father would like to invest.
He's asked me to do some investigating for him.
Can you give me any advice?
There are lots of books that you could read.
You may want to ask an advisor.

H. Listen to the reductions in the following conversation between a bank teller and a customer. Write the *long forms* in the blanks.

Teller: _____ _____ _____

_____ check your balance?

Customer: Yeah. _____ I'd _____

_____ know if my money has arrived from Japan.

Teller: All right. _____ _____ your account

number.

Customer: Here you are.

> *Teller:* Your balance is two hundred dollars. _____ your
>
> account doesn't show any deposits.
>
> *Customer:* Oh, no!
>
> *Teller:* Well, it takes a few days for the money to get here. Even a week,
>
> _____ _____ times. Come in
>
> again tomorrow. Or here's a number _____
>
> _____ can call.

Intonation

I. Listen to the following sentences. Concentrate on the words *can* and *can't*. In order
to hear the difference between the two forms, you must listen to the difference in
stress and *vowel sound*.

> You can buy a cheap house these days.
>   can búy
> You can't buy a cheap house these days.
>   cán't búy

Now repeat the following sentences.

Affirmative	*Negative*
We can lose money on the stockmarket.	We can't lose money on the stockmarket.
I can find my checkbook.	I can't find my checkbook.
Banks can charge 20 percent interest.	Banks can't charge 20 percent interest.
You can get cash.	You can't get cash.
Students can open a business.	Students can't open a business.

J. Listen to the sentences. Tell whether they are affirmative or negative. Circle *can*
or *can't*.

1. can   can't   6. can   can't

2. can   can't   7. can   can't

3. can   can't   8. can   can't

4. can   can't   9. can   can't

5. can   can't   10. can   can't

PART II. LECTURE

Above: the Apple Computer.

Left: a Federal Express delivery.

Context: The following lecture deals with a very important and interesting personality within the American business community: the entrepreneur.

Preview questions: Do you know the meaning of the words *entrepreneur* and its derivatives, *entrepreneurship, entrepreneurial?* When you think of successful American businesspeople, what personality characteristics do you usually think of to describe them? How are American businesspeople different from those in your native culture?

Vocabulary: The following terms appear in the lecture. Try to understand them from the context they are in; do not use a dictionary. After the lecture, you will be asked to write a brief definition of each term.

> to have something in common with someone
> entrepreneur, entrepreneurship
> risk (noun and verb)
> textile
> investment
> worth

A. Listen to the lecture. Follow the outline as you listen. Do not write anything at this point.

B. Listen again and fill in the outline.

OUTLINE

Entrepreneurs

I. Introduction: Three companies and the men who started them:

   A. Apple Computers — Steven Jobs

   B. _____ — Nolan Bushnell

   C. _____ — Frederick Smith

II. What these men have in common

   A. _____

   B. _____

   C. _____

   D. All are entrepreneurs

III. _____

   A. Definition: A person who _____

       _____

   B. Today, they can come from many backgrounds:

     1. Mostly young

     2. Some rich, some _____

     3. Some well-educated, others _____

   C. The thing they all have in common: _____

       _____

IV. _____

   A. Francis Cabot Lowell

     1. Started the first _____ factory in the United States

     2. Built his factory and sold cloth in _____

     3. Also made money by selling _____

   B. George Westinghouse

     1. In 1869, invented _____

     2. In 1886, started _____ ,

       which still exists today

   C. Edwin Land

     1. In 1837, started the Polaroid Corporation to make

2. In 1948, invented the Instamatic _____

V. Location of new industries

    A. Earlier in the century, industries depended on natural resources, transportation, manpower

    B. Today's industries are "high-tech"

        1. _____

        2. _____

        3. Genetic engineering

    C. Today's industries depend on _____

      As a result, they are located near _____

        1. Boston: M.I.T., Harvard

        2. "Silicon Valley"—San Francisco: Stanford, U.C. Berkeley

VI. Conclusion

    A. In 1975, _____ new businesses in U.S.

    B. In 1981, _____ new businesses—an increase of

    _____

    C. Americans respect entrepreneurship

    D. Entrepreneurs have become the new American cultural heroes

C. Listen to the following questions and write the answers.

    1. What personality traits do most entrepreneurs have in common?

      _____

      _____

      _____

    2. In what ways are entrepreneurs sometimes different from one another?

      _____

      _____

    3. What are high-tech industries? Why are they often located near universities?

      _____

      _____

4. Why do we say that entrepreneurs have become the new American cultural heroes?

_____

_____

D. *Vocabulary review.* Define these terms as they were used in the lecture.

1. to have something in common with someone: _____

_____

2. entrepreneur: _____

_____

3. entrepreneurship: _____

_____

4. risk: _____

_____

5. textile: _____

_____

6. investment: _____

_____

7. worth: _____

_____

PART III. MAKING INFERENCES

Most banks offer many different services. Look at the list of services below. Then listen to each advertisement and decide which service the speaker is talking about. Write the letter of the service in the blank. Then listen again and you will hear the correct answer.

a. a safety deposit box   e. an automated banking machine
b. a checking account   f. credit cards
c. a savings account   g. traveler's checks
d. a home improvement loan   h. car loans

1. The speaker is talking about _____ .

2. The speaker is talking about _____ .

3. The speaker is talking about _____ .

4. What can't the woman find? _____ .

5. The speaker is talking about _____ .

PART IV. LISTENING TASKS

George and Martha Spendthrift have a joint checking account. Here is one page from their checkbook record. Listen as they balance their checkbook. Fill in the missing information.

```
╔══════════════════════════════════════════════╗
        ═══════ CHECKBOOK RECORD ═══════
       NAME: George & Martha Spendthrift
       ACCOUNT: 132-98804
```

NO.	DATE	DESCRIPTION	PAYMENT	DEPOSIT	BALANCE
200	10/25		30.21		490.31
201	10/27	Electric Company	57.82		
202	10/27	Time Magazine			
203	10/30		70.00		327.49
204	11/1	Compu-Tech	125.00		202.49
205		Dr. Painless	40.00		162.49
	11/1	Deposit		1234.69	
206	11/2				985.18
207	11/4	Visa Payment	155.00		830.18
208	11/8		305.00		525.18
209	11/10	Traffic ticket			

PART V. SPEAKING ACTIVITIES

A. *Role-play.* In pairs or groups of three, act out the following situations.

1. You have applied for a credit card but the bank turned you down. Go to the bank and find out why. Here are some reasons the loan officer might give you:

   - You haven't lived here long enough.
   - Your income isn't high enough.
   - You didn't have good references.
   - You don't have an account with the bank.

   Ask the loan officer what to do in order to get a card.

2. You are an entrepreneur with some interesting business ideas but no money. Talk to one or more investors about the business you would like to start. Choose an area with great possibilities for the future—for example, genetic engineering, bionics, robotics, or space travel. Give the investor(s) reasons why this would be a good investment. The investor(s) should ask questions about the future business: How much capital is needed? How many employees will work in the business? When can the investor(s) expect a profit? What are the risks? etc.

B. *Pair work.* Below is a list of activities. Each of you tells your partner which things on the list you *can* or *can't* do. Use both *can* and *can't* in each sentence.

Example: I can cook but I can't sew.

Add other activities to the list. Then tell the class three things your partner can or can't do.

1. sew
2. cook
3. stand on my head
4. do a handstand
5. waterski
6. snow ski
7. sing in the shower
8. sing in front of people
9. speak _____ (your native language)

10. speak Latin
11. drive a car
12. pilot a plane
13. understand the teacher
14. understand the landlord
15. run a mile
16. run a marathon

C. *Discussion.*

1. In Part IV, a husband and wife quarrel about spending money. Who controls the family budget in *your* family? What is the general custom in your culture?

2. In the United States and Canada, almost everybody has one or more credit cards. Are credit cards very widely used in your native country? Why or why not? Do you have any credit cards? How difficult is it to get a credit card? Do you have to be married? Rich? Employed? A property owner?

3. Does your country have a tradition of entrepreneurship? How easy or difficult is it for an individual to start a new business in your country? If a person wants to start a new business, where will he or she go to get the money? If you had the money to start a business in your country now, what business would you choose and why?

4

JOBS AND PROFESSIONS

PART I. PHONOLOGICAL CLUES

Context: In the following dialogue, Linda, Jeff, and Gloria talk about job problems.
   Preview questions: Linda is a teacher; Jeff is a musician; Gloria is a student. What kind of job problems might each of them have?

Getting the Main Idea

A. Listen to the conversation. Listen for the main ideas only.

B. Discuss your answers to the preview questions. Were your predictions correct? What kind of job problems do Linda, Jeff, and Gloria have?

Stress

C. Listen to the conversation again and fill in the missing stressed words.

Gloria: What are you _____ ?

Jeff: My _____ hasn't been _____ much

lately. It _____ like I'll _____ to get

a _____-_____ job.

Gloria: _____ kind of _____ do you want to

_____ ?

Jeff: I don't really _____ . I've done _____

of _____ _____ . I've been a

_____ , a _____ driver,

a _____ . And _____ even worked in

a _____ chip factory!

Gloria: A _____ _____

_____ ?! What did you _____ there?

Jeff: I used to _____ the _____ chips

before they _____ into the _____ .

I _____ _____ the bad ones.

Gloria: That _____ like a _____

_____ _____ .

Jeff: It _____ _____ . And I haven't

_____ a _____

_____ chip since I _____

that _____ .

Linda: _____ so _____ ?

Jeff: _____ my _____ _____

at the _____ _____

_____ ?

Linda: Yeah. Actually, that _____ sound so _____

to me _____ _____ .

D. Now listen to the first part of the conversation again. Repeat each sentence after the speaker. Remember: stressed words are *louder and clearer* than unstressed words.

E. Listen to the rest of the conversation and write the important (stressed) words. Your notes should look like a telegram.

Gloria: _____

Linda: _____

_____

Gloria: _____

Linda: _____

Gloria: _____

Linda: _____

Jeff: _____

_____

_____

Linda: _____

Gloria: _____

_____

_____

Jeff: _____

_____

F. Using your notes, reconstruct the conversation with a partner, orally or in writing.

Reductions

G. Listen to these examples of long and short forms from the conversation and repeat the *short forms* after the speaker.

What are you doing?
I have to get a part-time job.
What kind of job do you want to get?
I've done lots of different things.
What did you do there?
I used to inspect potato chips.
I don't know.
I was going to be a writer.

H. Listen to the reductions in the following conversation between a factory manager and a job applicant. Write the *long forms* in the blanks.

Manager: I'm _____ _____ ask you some

questions, okay? What _____ _____

jobs have you had?

Applicant: I've had _____ _____ different jobs.

I _____ _____ work in a plastics

factory.

Manager: _____ _____ _____
do there?

Applicant: I _____ _____ cut sheets of plastic.

Manager: _____ _____ _____
_____ _____ do here?

Applicant: I _____ _____ , . . . I'll do anything
. . . I'm broke, I _____ _____ make
some money right away.

Manager: Well, it looks like we're _____ _____
have an opening next week. I'll call you.

Applicant: Thanks.

PART II. LECTURE

Member of the United Garment Workers.

Members of the Farmworkers of America.

Member of the United Auto Workers.   *Teamsters Union worker.*

Context: The following short talk contains information about workers' organizations in the United States, called labor unions.

Preview questions: What do you think is the purpose of a labor union? What are some benefits workers may receive in addition to their salaries?

Vocabulary: The following terms appear in the lecture. Try to understand them from the context they are in; do not use a dictionary. After the lecture, you will be asked to write a brief definition of each term.

> labor
> union
> management
> wages
> security
> bargain, bargaining
> negotiate

A. Listen to the lecture. Follow the outline as you listen. Do not write anything at this point.

B. Listen again and fill in the outline.

OUTLINE
Labor Unions

I. Introduction

   A. Before labor unions, workers didn't have power

   B. In the 1930s, _____

     _____

   C. Today, about one-fourth of nonagricultural workers in the United States_____

     _____

      1. Largest number in _____ ,

     _____ , and _____ industries

      2. All together there are more than _____ unions

II. Labor unions

   A. The purpose of unions: to improve working conditions for its

     _____

   B. Goals of management: keep costs down and

     _____

   C. _____ and _____ must work together.
     This process is _____

III. During a _____

   A. Labor representative presents _____

      1. Wages

      2. _____

      3. _____

      4. Fringe Benefits

   B. _____ makes different offer

   C. The two sides _____

   D. They consult _____

   E. In the end they write a _____

IV. Contents of a labor contract

   A. _____

      1. Workers are paid by the hour or by the number of pieces

2. _____

B. _____ : advantages a worker enjoys

  1. Examples:

    a. Medical insurance

    b. Dental insurance

    c. _____

    d. _____

    e. _____

  2. Important because people don't have to _____

C. Seniority

  1. Definition: _____

    _____

  2. If company has to lay off people, it first lays off the ones with _____

D. _____ for workplace

  1. _____

  2. Protective clothing

V. Unions are important to American workers

C. Listen to the following questions and write the answers.

  1. What was the situation of American workers like before the 1930s? _____

    _____

  2. Do most workers in the United States belong to unions? _____

  3. What are some examples of well-known labor unions? _____

    _____

  4. What is the purpose of labor unions? _____

    _____

  5. What subjects do most labor contracts cover? _____

D. *Vocabulary review.* Define these terms as they were used in the lecture.

  1. labor: _____

    _____

  2. union: _____

    _____

3. management: _____

_____

4. wages: _____

_____

5. security: _____

_____

6. bargain: _____

_____

7. negotiate: _____

_____

PART III. MAKING INFERENCES

Read the list of occupations. Make sure you understand what each one is before you listen to the conversations. As you listen, decide what each speaker's job is and write the letter of the job in the blank. Then listen again and you will hear the correct answer.

a. secretary	g. medical receptionist
b. restaurant hostess	h. computer salesman
c. architect	i. plumber
d. construction worker	j. tailor
e. accountant	k. airline hostess
f. dentist	l. police officer

1. What's the woman's job? _____   **4.** What's the man's job? _____

2. What's the woman's job? _____   **5.** What's the man's job? _____

3. What's the woman's job? _____

PART IV. LISTENING TASK

People used to think that women who stayed home and took care of their children were not real members of the labor force. A housewife was "just" a housewife. Today we recognize that housewives often work as much as sixty hours a week (without pay!) and have a variety of skills.

You are going to hear one housewife describe a typical workday. *Some* of her activities are shown in the pictures below. Before you listen, look at the pictures. Describe each activity. Then listen to the monologue several times. Number the pictures in the correct order. Activities that happened at the same time should have the same number.

PART V. SPEAKING ACTIVITIES

A. *Role-play.*

1. There is a job opening in a supermarket and there are three applicants for the job. Three students in your class volunteer to play the part of the applicants. As a class, interview each applicant separately. (Two should wait outside while the class interviews one.) You may ask the same questions of all three, or your questions may vary. Then decide which applicant should get the job. Give your reasons.

B. *Activities.*

1. Think of a job. One person gets up in front of the class and pantomimes (acts out without words) the job. The student who guesses correctly gets to pantomime next.

2. "Twenty Questions." One person thinks of a job but does not tell the class what it is. The class tries to guess it by asking yes/no questions. Examples: "Can you do this job outdoors?" "Do you need a college education for this job?" The student who guesses correctly wins. If no one guesses after twenty questions, the person who thought of the job gets to play one more round.

C. *Discussion.*

1. In Part I, Gloria complains that she can't work in the United States because she is a foreign student. Do you think this law is fair? What might be the reasons for this law?

2. In Part I, Linda is thinking of changing careers. Do people in your country change jobs or careers easily?

3. In this country many teenagers have part-time jobs. What are the advantages and disadvantages for teenagers of working part time?

5

LIFESTYLES

PART I. PHONOLOGICAL CLUES

Context: Jeff is babysitting for Margie, who is a single mother.

   Preview questions: What do you think "single mother" means? Are there many "single mothers" in your country? What do you think of men taking care of babies?

Getting the Main Idea

A. Listen to the conversation. Listen to the main ideas only.

B. Discuss your answers to the preview questions. Were your predictions correct? How does Gloria feel about being a single mother? How about Linda?

Stress

C. In most two- and three-word verbs, especially nonseparable ones, the *second* word receives the stress.

Examples: The plane **took off′** at seven o'clock.
John **takes care′ of** his mother.
Please **drop** me **off′** at the corner.

Listen to the following examples of two- and three-word verbs from the conversation. Fill in the blanks with the missing stressed words.

1. Come _____ .

2. They have a problem and want me to look _____ it right away.

3. He probably won't wake _____ before I get

   _____ .

4. Listen, I've got to take _____ .

5. Thanks for helping me _____ .

6. I take _____ of him from time to time.

7. I've run _____ several unmarried women with kids.

8. I'm thirty-five now and time is running _____ .

9. I could never bring _____ a child by myself.

10. I'd better check _____ on Joey.

D. Now listen to the ten sentences again. Repeat each sentence after the speaker. Remember: stressed words are *louder and clearer* than unstressed words.

PART II. LECTURE

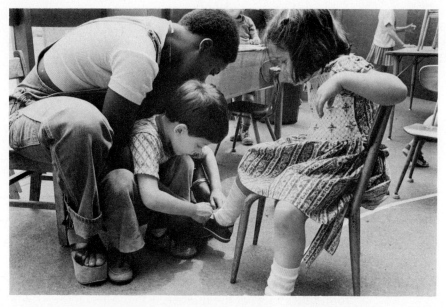

A child learns to tie a shoelace in a day-care center in Massachusetts.

Context: The following lecture is about changes in the structure of the American family. The lecture also discusses the response of business to these changes.

Preview questions: Can you give the definition of the "traditional American family"? What do you know about changes in the traditional American family? What might be the reasons for some of these changes?

Vocabulary: The following terms appear in the lecture. Try to understand them from the context they are in; do not use a dictionary. After the lecture, you will be asked to write a brief definition of each term.

single-parent families	maternity leave
labor force	flextime
household	day-care centers
homemaker	job sharing

A. Listen to the lecture. Follow the outline as you listen. Do not write anything at this point.

B. Listen again and fill in the outline.

OUTLINE

Changes in the American Family

I. Introduction

    A. Traditional American family: _____ , _____ ,

       and _____

    B. Examples of new kinds of families:

       1. Single mothers and fathers

       2. _____

       3. _____

       4. _____

II. Social and economic reasons for change

    A. _____

    B. _____

    C. (Most important) _____

III. New problems for American family

    A. _____

    B. _____

    C. _____

IV. Not just "women's problems"

V. Corporations, labor unions and government have created new policies to help working parents

    A. _____

    B. _____

    C. _____

    D. _____

    E. _____

    F. _____

    G. _____

VI. In spite of new business policies, most working parents still have trouble finding time for both their jobs and their families

C. Listen to the following questions and write the answers.

    1. What is the traditional American family like?

       _____

       _____

       _____

    2. What are two reasons for the changing American family pattern?

       _____

       _____

    3. What are some new problems for the American family?

       _____

       _____

       _____

    4. What are three examples of how businesses respond to the needs of working parents?

       _____

       _____

       _____

       _____

D. *Vocabulary review.* Define these terms as they were used in the lecture.

1. single-parent families: _____

   _____

2. labor force: _____

   _____

3. household: _____

   _____

4. homemaker: _____

   _____

5. maternity leave: _____

   _____

6. flextime: _____

   _____

7. day-care centers: _____

   _____

8. job sharing: _____

   _____

PART III. MAKING INFERENCES

Listen to the following people talking about their lifestyles. Decide who the speakers are and circle the best answer. Then listen again. This time you will hear the correct answer.

1. a. factory worker
   b. retired person
   c. landlord

2. a. the police
   b. teachers
   c. parents

3. a. has never been married
   b. is divorced
   c. is married now

4. a. with his parents
    b. alone
    c. with roommates

5. a. a retirement home
    b. a house with friends
    c. a hospital

PART IV. LISTENING TASK

Below are three incomplete graphs. In each case, the numbers at the bottom represent years and the numbers on the left represent percentages. Listen to the information. Use it to fill in the graphs. The first item is done for you.

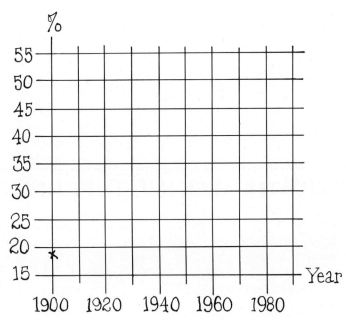

PERCENTAGE OF WOMEN IN WORKING POPULATION

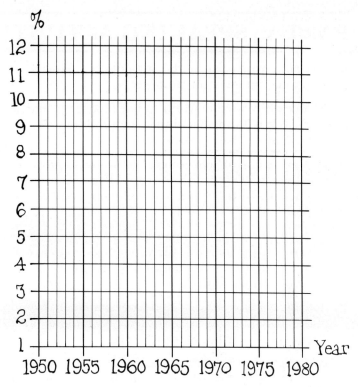

%

U.S. DIVORCE RATE BETWEEN 1950 AND 1980

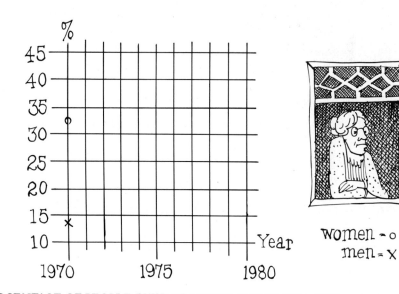

women = o
men = x

PERCENTAGE OF PEOPLE OVER 65 LIVING ALONE 1970–1980

PART V. SPEAKING ACTIVITIES

A. *Role-play.* With a partner(s), act out the following situations. Each skit should end with a resolution of the problem.

1. An elderly woman wants to live alone; her married son and his wife insist that she live with them and their two children. The son and mother each give reasons for their preferences.

2. A nineteen-year-old college girl wants to move out of her parents' home, although she goes to a nearby college. She has a job, so she can support herself. The parents feel it is a waste of money. Each gives a reason for his or her position.

3. A young man and woman have been going together for eight months. The man wants to get married; the woman wants to live with him without marriage. The man tries to persuade her to get married while she gives reasons why she would rather wait.

B. *Activity: Opinion survey.* Choose one statement from the list below. Ask *each member* of the class if they agree or disagree with the statement. Take notes on each answer. Then report your findings to the class.

Example: "Twelve students agreed that children should live with their mothers after a divorce. Three people disagreed, and one person was unsure."

1. Men and women shouldn't live together before marriage.

2. A woman's place is in the home.

3. Two is the ideal number of children in a family.

4. It's unnatural for married people to decide not to have children.

5. Children are responsible for taking care of their elderly parents.

6. Children should live with their parents until they get married.

7. It's better for children to live with one parent than with two who don't get along.

8. In the event of divorce, children should live with their mothers.

9. People over sixty-five should not drive.

10. People should have to retire at age sixty-five.

11. Young people should have to get their parents' permission in order to get married.

12. Public schools should teach sex education.

13. It's not good for a wife to earn more money than her husband.

14. Interracial marriages are bad because the children will suffer.

15. The government should finance day-care centers.

16. It's better for adopted children not to find out who their real parents were.

17. In overpopulated countries, the government has the right to limit the number of children a family has.

18. Sometimes it's good for married couples to take separate vacations.

C. *Discussion.*

1. In Part III you heard the following five speakers:
   a. a retired person on a fixed income
   b. a teenager living with her parents
   c. a single father
   d. an adult moving back to his parents' home
   e. a retirement-home resident

   What were their problems? Are their problems common in your country?

2. Look at the three graphs in Part IV. What trends in our society do they illustrate? What may be some reasons for these trends? For example, why are there so many more elderly women than men living alone? Why was the divorce rate so low in the 1950s?

6
TRAVEL AND
TRANSPORTATION

PART I. PHONOLOGICAL CLUES

Context: Gloria and her classmate Ming are planning to visit San Francisco. Linda, who knows the city very well, gives them some advice.

    Preview questions: Pretend that Gloria and Ming live in your town. What type of travel

plans would they have to make? How much do you know about San Francisco and its transportation system?

Getting the Main Idea

A. Listen to the conversation. Listen for the main ideas only.

B. Discuss your answers to the preview questions. Were your predictions correct? What did Gloria and Ming need to know about San Francisco? What did they learn about getting around in San Francisco?

Stress

C. Listen to the conversation again and fill in the missing stressed words.

Gloria: Linda, _____ remember my friend

_____ ?

Linda: _____ , I _____ you at

_____ . How _____ you?

Ming: Fine, thanks.

Gloria: Ming and I are going to take a _____ to

_____ _____ together during the

_____ . Do you _____ if we

_____ you some _____ ?

Linda: Of _____ not. I _____ that city.

What do you want to _____ ?

Ming: Well, _____ of all, we're not _____

how to _____ there. Should we go by

_____ , by _____ , by

_____ . . . ?

Linda: That _____ . _____ you have enough

_____ but not much _____ , it'll be

best to _____ . The _____ isn't much

_____ , but if you take the _____ ,

you can see the _____ along the

_____ .

Gloria: But what about the _____ ?

Linda: Well, the _____ is the _____ , but it's

_____ too _____ . It's

_____ kind of _____ .

Ming: We don't have to _____ too much about

_____ because we'll be _____ with

my _____ in _____ . On

the _____ hand, we don't have that much

_____—only two _____ .

Gloria: I _____ we'd better _____ then. But

_____ will we get _____

when we _____ there?

Linda: In _____ _____

_____ is no _____ . The

whole _____ is only _____ square

_____ , so you can _____ to

a _____ of _____ .

There is an _____ bus system.

D. Now listen to the first part of the conversation again. Repeat each sentence after the speaker. Remember: stressed words are *louder and clearer* than unstressed words.

E. Listen to the rest of the conversation and write the important (stressed) words. Your notes should look like a telegram.

Ming: _____

Linda: _____

_____

_____

Gloria: _____

Linda: _____

_____

Ming: _____

Linda: _____

_____

Gloria: _____

Linda: _____

_____

_____

Gloria: _____

Linda: _____

Gloria: _____

Linda: _____

F. Using your notes, reconstruct the conversation with a partner, orally or in writing.

Reductions

G. Listen to these examples of long and short forms from the conversation and repeat the *short forms* after the speaker.

Yes, I met you at school.

Ming and I are going to take a trip to San Francisco.

Do you mind if we ask you some questions?

What do you want to know?

You can see the country along the way.

It's also kind of slow.

You can walk to a lot of places.

Another thing you guys ought to do is take the ferry.

Why don't you come with us?

H. Now listen to the reductions in the following conversation between an airline ticket agent and a customer. Write the *long forms* in the blanks.

Customer: Hi. I _____ _____ make reservations

for a flight to Cairo.

Agent: When _____ _____

_____ _____ leave?

Customer: Tomorrow.

Agent: Tomorrow? That's _____ _____

difficult. All our flights are booked 'til next Monday.

Customer: Oh, no! _____ _____ have anything

sooner?

Agent: I'm afraid not.

Customer: What am I _____ _____ do?

Agent: You _____ _____ call another

airline.

PART II. LECTURE

Context: You are going to hear a lecture on transportation in the twenty-first century.

  Preview questions: What methods of transportation are most common today? How do you imagine they will change in the next hundred years?

  Vocabulary: The following terms appear in the lecture. Try to understand them from the context they are in; do not use a dictionary. After the lecture, you will be asked to write a brief definition of each term.

supersonic speed	rapid transit systems
modes of transportation	"people movers"
to program	train tracks
fuel	pilot

A. Listen to the lecture. Follow the outline as you listen. Do not write anything at this point.

B. Listen again and fill in the outline.

OUTLINE

_____

I. Introduction

   A. The example about the businessman is to show:

     _____

     _____

   B. The lecture topic: _____

II. _____

   A. Will be the most important method of traveling

   B. Will improve in the following ways:

     1. _____

     2. _____

     3. Cars will be smaller and _____

       a. Will still use _____

       b. Mileage will be _____

III. Transportation in _____

   A. _____

   B. Buses

     1. _____

     2. will look different from buses today

     3. _____

     4. _____

   C. _____

     1. _____

     2. Exist today in _____

IV. Long-distance traveling

   A. _____ will be more comfortable

     1. sleeper seats

     2. _____

     3. _____

4. _____

B. _____

    1. Will travel _____ the tracks, not on them

    2. Very fast: _____ per hour

V. _____

    A. Constructed of _____

        1. _____

        2. _____

        3. cleaner

        4. _____

    B. Larger—1000 passengers

    C. _____

    D. In the passenger area:

        1. _____

        2. _____

VI. Conclusion _____

C. Listen to the following questions and write the answers.

  1. How will cars change in the next fifty to one hundred years?

    _____

    _____

    _____

  2. What type of rapid transit systems will people use in the future?

    _____

    _____

    _____

  3. According to the lecture, which two modes of transportation will computers control?

    _____

    _____

  4. What will be the cheapest way to travel long distances?

D. *Vocabulary review.* Define these terms as they were used in the lecture.

1. supersonic speed: _____

_____

2. modes of transportation: _____

_____

3. to program: _____

_____

4. fuel: _____

_____

5. rapid transit system: _____

_____

6. "people movers": _____

_____

7. train tracks: _____

_____

8. pilot: _____

_____

PART III. MAKING INFERENCES

Each of these conversations deals with a travel problem. Listen to the speakers and decide what the problem is. After each conversation you will hear a question. Circle the best answer. Then listen again. This time you will hear the correct answer.

1. a. The woman lost her purse.
   b. She locked the car keys in the car.
   c. Their car broke down.

2. a. She lost her luggage.
   b. She lost her ticket.
   c. She missed her plane.

3. a. She was smoking.

b. She was blocking the door.
c. She was not wearing her seatbelt.

4. a. She is pregnant.
   b. She is tired.
   c. She is seasick.

5. a. The airport is closed.
   b. Traffic is too heavy.
   c. It's snowing in New York.

PART IV. LISTENING TASK

A. When you own a car, you have to remember many things. If you forget anything, then possibly other things will happen. These are *causes* and *effects*.

Read the ten *effects* below and make sure you understand them. Listen to ten *causes* beginning with *if* and match them with the correct *effects* beginning with *then*. Choose the correct letter and write it next to the number.

If . . .	**Then . . .**
1. _g_	a. you will be able to see clearly
2. ____	b. your motor will not overheat
3. ____	c. the motor will run smoothly
4. ____	d. you may lose control of your car
5. ____	e. you will be safer in an accident
6. ____	f. a flat tire will not be a disaster
7. ____	g. someone might steal it
8. ____	h. you will see the traffic behind you
9. ____	i. your battery will be dead
10. ____	j. you might get a ticket

B. Listen to the description of each part of the car. Write the names of the parts in the correct places on the picture of the car on the next page.

Parts of the Car

hood	headlight
tire	trunk
windshield	fender
license plate	bumper

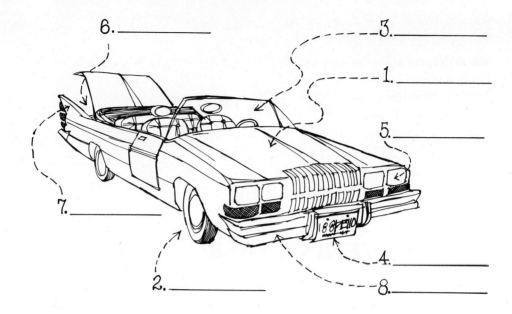

6. _____

3. _____

1. _____

5. _____

7. _____

2. _____

4. _____

8. _____

PART V. SPEAKING ACTIVITIES

A. *Role-play.* With a partner(s), act out the following situations. Each skit should end with a resolution of the problem.

1. A passenger on a train or plane approaches you and rudely tells you that you are sitting in his or her seat. The attendant interrupts and asks to see both your tickets. Resolve the situation: Whose seat is it? Will you have to move?

2. A police officer stops you for speeding on a highway. He says you were going sixty-five miles per hour in a fifty-five-mile-per-hour zone. Try to talk the police officer out of giving you a ticket.

3. You have ordered a special vegetarian dinner on an airplane. The stewardess brings you the wrong meal. Complain and ask her to bring you the correct meal.

4. You are on a flight from Puerto Rico to Miami. In the middle of the flight, a man suddenly jumps from his seat and announces that he is hijacking the plane to Cuba. While everyone else panics, you keep cool and try to talk the man out of hijacking the plane.

B. *Activities: telephone practice.*

1. Decide on a North American city you'd like to visit. Call your local train station, the airlines, and a long-distance bus company to find out how much it

costs to get there. Then, figure out how much you will spend on gasoline if you decide to drive. Which way is the cheapest?

2. What are the requirements for getting a driver's license in your state or area (minimum age, maximum age, costs, frequency of renewal, permits, etc.)? Call your local motor vehicle office and report your findings to the class.

C. *Discussion.*

1. Discuss the advantages and disadvantages for the worker and his or her family of the following jobs in transportation. Would you like to have one of the jobs? Which one and why?

airline pilot	train engineer
steward/stewardess	bus driver
cab driver	boat captain
truck driver	air-traffic controller
travel agent	

2. Are there many traffic problems in the city or town you come from? What about in the place where you live now? If there are any problems, do you know of any plans to solve them or do you have any ideas for solving them?

3. If space travel becomes possible and affordable for everyone within your lifetime, will you go? Why or why not?

4. Tell about an interesting or unusual travel experience you have had.

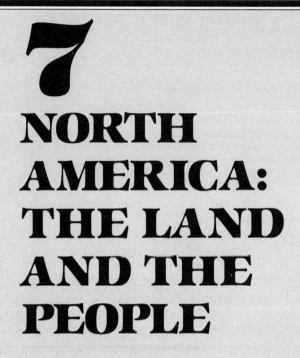

7

NORTH AMERICA: THE LAND AND THE PEOPLE

PART I. PHONOLOGICAL CLUES

Context: Gloria and Ming are having lunch in a crowded cafeteria in downtown San Francisco. In the following conversation, they make a new acquaintance and talk with him about the people of San Francisco.

Preview questions: What are ethnic groups? What's the ethnic composition of your city? Do you know the ethnic composition of San Francisco?

Getting the Main Idea

A. Listen to the conversation. Listen for the main ideas only.

B. Discuss your answers to the preview questions. Were your predictions correct? What did Gloria and Ming find out about the people of San Francisco?

Stress

C. Listen to the conversation again and fill in the missing stressed words.

Man: So you're _____ San Francisco?

Gloria: Yes, we just _____ here _____

_____ . And _____ ?

Man: I'm a _____ .

Ming: Oh, _____ ? Everyone _____ we've

_____ so far has been a _____ like

_____ . I was _____ to

_____ that there _____ no

_____ .

Man: Well, San Francisco has a _____ of different

_____ _____ , so you might

_____ you're seeing a lot of _____ .

But actually, the _____ has a _____

of about _____ .

Gloria: What are the different _____ _____ ?

Man: Well, after _____ , the _____ one is

_____ .

Gloria: _____ thought it was _____ .

Man: It's _____ that San Francisco has the

_____ Chinese community _____

of _____ . But there are many more

_____ here than _____ .

Ming: That's _____ . Don't _____ of the

_____ people live in _____ ?

Man: Well, no, they live _____ _____ the

Above: in San Francisco's Mission District, people attend theaters with films in Spanish.

Right: a typical street in Chinatown, San Francisco.

city, but _____ is _____ the center of

Chinese _____ here. _____ where

you'll find the _____ Chinese _____ ,

_____ , _____ ,

_____ , things like that.

D. Now listen to the first part of the conversation again. Repeat each sentence after the speaker. Remember: stressed words are *louder and clearer* than unstressed words.

E. Listen to the rest of the conversation and write the important (stressed) words. Your notes should look like a telegram.

Gloria: _____

Man: _____

_____

Ming: _____

Man: _____

_____

Gloria: _____

Man: _____

_____

Ming: _____

Man: _____

_____

Ming: _____

Gloria: _____

F. Using your notes, reconstruct the conversation with a partner, orally or in writing.

Intonation

G. Listen to the following exchange from the conversation.

> *Man:* So you're visiting San Francisco?

> *Gloria:* Yes, we just got here last night.

Notice that the man's question is actually a statement, *You are visiting San Francisco,* with rising intonation. Statements with rising intonation are often used in rapid, informal English, especially when one is surprised or expects an affirmative answer. Listen to the following "statement questions" and change them into "true" questions.

Example: So, you're visiting San Francisco?

So, are you visiting San Francisco?

1. _____

2. _____

3. _____

4. _____

PART II. LECTURE

Context: This chapter deals with the land and people of North America, including both the United States and Canada. In this lecture you will learn a little about differences in the way people throughout North America speak the English language.

Differences in the ethnic groups that settled various parts of North America partly determined regional differences in speech. In the southwest of the United States, the Hispanic influence is widespread.

In parts of Canada, French influence is strong and there are two official languages, English and French.

Preview questions: Have you traveled much in North America? Which places have you visited? Did you notice anything special about the way people there speak English? Was it difficult for you to understand them? In your country, do people speak the language differently from one region to the next? Do people from different regions have any trouble understanding one another?

Vocabulary: The following terms appear in the lecture. Try to understand them from the context they are in; do not use a dictionary. After the lecture, you will be asked to write a brief definition of each term.

continent	features	lexicon	variation
region	standard	obvious	

A. Listen to the lecture. Follow the outline as you listen. Do not write anything at this point.

B. Listen again and fill in the outline.

OUTLINE
Differences in North American English

I. People in different regions of North America speak English differently. Differences in:

    A. Pronunciation

    B. _____

    C. _____

II. Differences in _____

    A. Canadians _____

       Example words: _____ , _____ ,

       _____

    B. _____ add an /r/ in words such as:

       1. _____

       2. _____

       3. _____

    C. Bostonians:

       1. Pronunce /a/ like _____ : e.g., /aant/

       2. Drop most _____ , e.g., /pahk the cah/

III. Differences in _____

    A. Written grammar the same everywhere

    B. Differences in _____ . Examples:

       1. _____

       2. Confusion between *it is* and *there is*

IV. Differences in _____

    A. Examples:

       1. _____

       2. _____

       3. _____

    B. Lexical differences in North America are determined by

_____ , not by social or educational class

V. Conclusion: There are hundreds of differences, but _____

_____

C. Listen to the following questions and write the answers.

1. What are the three components of spoken English, as discussed in this lecture?

_____

_____

2. What is meant by *standard* English?

_____

3. Why is there less variation in grammar than in pronunciation and vocabulary?

_____

_____

4. Do Americans and Canadians understand each other's English?

_____

D. *Vocabulary review.* Define these terms as they were used in the lecture.

1. continent: _____

_____

2. region: _____

_____

3. features: _____

_____

4. standard: _____

_____

5. lexicon: _____

_____

6. obvious: _____

_____

7. variation: _____

_____

PART III. MAKING INFERENCES

Listen to the following information about the United States and Canada. Draw conclusions based on the facts you hear. Pay special attention to numbers and percentages. Circle the best answer. You will hear each item twice.

1. a. rising
   b. falling
   c. staying the same

2. a. Canada is larger than the United States
   b. Puerto Rico is probably rather crowded.
   c. The United States has many immigrants from Puerto Rico.

3. a. "the sunbelt"
   b. "the breadbasket of the nation"
   c. "the Wild West"

4. a. getting ready for bed
   b. eating breakfast
   c. coming home from work.

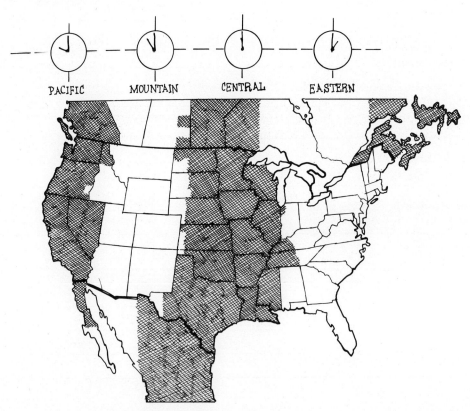

5. a. English as a Second Language is an important subject in L.A. public schools.
   b. Los Angeles has many immigrants from India.
   c. Los Angeles public schools don't teach English well.

PART IV. LISTENING TASK

Look at the map of North America. Familiarize yourself with the information you see. You will hear some *true* and some *false* statements about U.S. and Canadian geography. Write T for *true* and F for *false* based on what the map tells you.

1. _____	6. _____	11. _____
2. _____	7. _____	12. _____
3. _____	8. _____	13. _____
4. _____	9. _____	14. _____
5. _____	10. _____	15. _____

PART V. SPEAKING ACTIVITIES

A. *Activities.*

1. Your English teacher has received good teaching job offers in four major U.S. cities. The pay and benefits are the same for all four jobs. Help your teacher decide which of the following cities to choose: Boston, Denver, Seattle, New Orleans.
   In teams, investigate the following aspects of each city:

   - climate
   - industry/pollution
   - population
   - geographic features
   - number of foreigners
   - cultural activities (symphony, museums, sports)

   You may want to consult an almanac or encyclopedia.

2. Turn back to Part IV and listen to the statements on the tape again. Use the map and correct all *false* statements.

   Example: (for Number 7) The primary product of Wisconsin isn't fruit; it's cheese. Fruit is the primary product of California.

B. *Discussion.*

1. Before you came to this country, what ideas did you have about Americans or Canadians? For instance, what expectations did you have about their behavior, lifestyles, attitudes, customs, habits? Make a list of your ideas before you begin your discussion.

2. How have your ideas changed since you came to this country? What specific things caused them to change (e.g., experiences you've had, people you have talked to, articles you have read, and so forth).

3. Summarize what you have learned about the United States and Canada in this chapter, specifically about:

- language
- ethnic groups
- geography
- crops and industries
- climate

Add any other knowledge you have to your summary of each of these points.

8

TASTES AND PREFERENCES

PART I. PHONOLOGICAL CLUES

Context: In the following conversation Gloria gets to know Dan, Jeff's musician friend. They are trying to find out what they have in common.

Preview questions: What kind of questions might Gloria and Dan ask each other? Is it important for two people to have the same tastes in order to get along?

Getting the Main Idea

A. Listen to the conversation. Listen for the main ideas only.

B. Discuss your answers to the preview questions. Were your predictions correct? What did Dan and Gloria find out about each other?

Stress

C. Listen to the conversation again and fill in the missing stressed words.

    Jeff: Come _____ .

    Dan: Hi.

  Gloria: Oh _____ , Dan, how _____ you?

    Jeff: Hey, Dan! How're you _____ ?

    Dan: Everything is _____ . I brought some

           _____ for you to _____ to.

    Jeff: Great. Oh, _____ the _____ .

_____ be _____

_____ .

Gloria: Okay.

Dan: So, _____ did you _____ of our

_____ last night?

Gloria: Your _____ solo in the _____ song

was _____ .

Dan: Thanks. But _____ did you _____ of

the _____ of our music?

Gloria: Well, it's _____ for _____ but, to tell

you the _____ , loud music _____

my _____ . I guess I _____

_____ music.

Dan: Do you go to _____ very much?

Gloria: No, not _____ often. I _____

_____ it. They're _____ expensive.

Dan: So, _____ do you like to do for

_____ ?

Gloria: Well, I love to _____ . There're

_____ many _____ ethnic

restaurants in this _____ .

D. Now listen to the first part of the conversation again. Repeat each sentence after the speaker. Remember: stressed words are *louder and clearer* than unstressed words.

E. Listen to the rest of the conversation and write the important (stressed) words. Your notes should look like a telegram.

Dan: _____

Gloria: _____

Dan: _____

_____

Gloria: _____

Dan: _____

Gloria: _____

Dan: _____
Gloria: _____
Dan: _____
Gloria: _____
Dan: _____
Gloria: _____
Dan: _____

Gloria: _____
Dan: _____
Gloria: _____

F. Using your notes, reconstruct the conversation with a partner, orally or in writing.

Intonation

G. Listen to this exchange from the conversation.

> *Dan:* Do you like football?
>
> *Gloria:* I hate it.
>
> *Dan:* Basketball?

Notice the form of Dan's second question. How can you tell that it's a question? Which words are missing? How do you know? The complete question should be "Do you like basketball?" Dan drops the subject and the verb "Do you like" because his meaning is clear to Gloria from the context of the first question. This kind of reduction is common in rapid, informal speech. Listen to the following short exchanges. Write the full question instead of the reduced question.

Example: __*Do you like*__ Japanese __*food*__ ?

1. _____ tired?
2. _____ anybody home?
3. _____ leaving already?
4. _____ kids?

PART II. LECTURE

Context: This lecture is about a segment of the American population known as the "baby-boom generation." You will learn who they are, what they are like, and why they are important to the American economy.

Preview questions: Can you guess the meaning of the term "baby boom"? Is the population of the United States basically "young," "middle-aged," or "old"? In what way do you think this fact is important to American business and industry? What is the age distribution like in your country, compared to the United States?

Vocabulary: The following terms appear in the lecture. Try to understand them from the context they are in; do not use a dictionary. After the lecture, you will be asked to write a brief definition of each term.

birth rate	credit
baby boom	factor
affluence	middle age

A. Listen to the lecture. Follow the outline as you listen. Do not write anything at this point.

B. Listen again and fill in the outline.

Left, opposite page: young "baby boomers" in the 1950s.

Right, opposite page: adolescent members of the baby-boom generation in the 1960s.

Left: in the 1980s, "baby boomers" are having a large impact on business, including businesses related to housing.

OUTLINE

The Baby-Boom Generation

I. Between the end of World War II and the mid-1960s, the U.S. birthrate

_____

   A. Americans call this period the _____

   B. The oldest baby boomers are now _____ years old

II. Most powerful economic group has always been people between

_____

   A. Number of families in this age group is increasing:

      1. 1979 _____

      2. 1985 _____

      3. 1990 _____

   B. Reason for increase: _____

III. 35–44 is also becoming _____

   A. Average household income, 1990 _____

B. Total spending power will grow by _____

C. *Time Magazine* concludes: _____ and _____ of

    35–44 group make it most important economic factor of 1980s.

IV. Other influencing factors:

A. The boom started after _____ , during times of

    _____ . As a result, "baby boomers" _____ their

    money instead of _____

B. Major users of _____

C. Grew up in _____

D. Have more _____

V. Business and industry have changed because of this group

Examples:

A. Biggest expense: _____

    1. Spend a lot of money on _____

    2. Increase in the 35–44 group benefited _____

    _____

B. Interested in _____

    1. Cars should be _____

    2. Also interested in _____

    3. Group buys many _____

    4. _____ industry has profited from increase in this group

C. 35–44 group interested in _____

    1. Result: increase in number of _____

D. Some industries creating products specifically for middle-aged people:

    1. Levi's: _____

    2. Mattel: _____

    3. _____

VI. In the future, _____

_____

C. Listen to the following questions and write the answers.

1. Is the U.S. population getting older, younger, or staying the same?

   _____

2. How does the baby-boom generation spend its money differently from the way their parents did?

   _____

   _____

   _____

3. How is industry responding? Give specific examples.

   _____

   _____

   _____

D. *Vocabulary review.* Define these terms as they were used in the lecture.

1. birth rate: _____

   _____

2. baby boom: _____

   _____

3. affluence: _____

   _____

4. credit: _____

   _____

5. factor: _____

   _____

6. middle age: _____

   _____

PART III. MAKING INFERENCES

Listen to each of the following conversations. Decide what the speakers are talking about. Circle the best answer. Then listen to the conversation again. This time you will hear the correct answer.

1. a. a car
   b. a painting
   c. a movie

2. a. T-shirt
   b. tie
   c. pair of shoes

3. a. dance
   b. waterski
   c. jump

4. a. He likes it.
   b. He is not sure.
   c. He thinks it's funny.

5. a. He likes it.
   b. He is not sure.
   c. He thinks it's funny.

PART IV. LISTENING TASK

David is a thirty-year-old professional. For the last year, David has had two girlfriends, Nancy and Jean. He likes both of them very much. Both women are interested in him, but David is having a hard time choosing between them. Listen as David describes both women. As he talks, list their positive and negative qualities in the chart below. Listen as often as necessary.

Nancy		**Jean**	
+	−	+	−

Compare your list with your neighbors'. What do you think David should do?

PART V. SPEAKING ACTIVITIES

A. *Role-play*. With a partner(s), act out the following situations. Each skit should end with a resolution of the problem.

1. A man can't choose between two girlfriends (or a woman between two boyfriends). He or she goes to a psychologist and lists the positive and negative qualities of both. The psychologist helps him or her decide.

2. Two people are on their first date. They ask and answer questions regarding taste in cars, music, favorite colors, etc. On the basis of the answers, they decide whether they will have a second date.

3. A husband and wife are shopping for a car. He wants one type (for example, a sports model), she wants another (for example, a station wagon). They both make a case for the one they want, based on logic and their preferences. Finally, they make a decision.

B. *Activities.*

1. Write an ad about yourself for a singles magazine. List your best qualities. Do not write your name on it. Your teacher will collect and type up each ad and give one copy to each student. Guess which ad fits which person.

2. "Academy Awards" game. Nominate people and places that are familiar to everyone in the class. Categories:

    - most beautiful woman
    - most handsome man
    - best athlete
    - best restaurant in this town
    - best student in this class
    - best vacation spot
    - best movie of the year
    - best singer, athlete
    - (any other categories you may want to add)

Write the nominees on the blackboard. Then vote for one winner in each category.

C. *Discussion.*

1. What qualities are important to you in a mate?

2. What's your favorite thing to do on a Saturday night? Sunday afternoon? Would your choice be different in your native country?

3. What is your favorite city in the world? Why? Be specific.

4. What are some things that are considered good taste in your culture but bad taste here and vice versa (for example, eating with one's hands)?

5. Do people from the same culture have similar tastes in most things or is taste completely individual?

9
THE SKY ABOVE US

PART I. PHONOLOGICAL CLUES

Context: Linda, Jeff, and Gloria are talking about space travel and exploration.

Preview questions: Which one of the three might be the most adventurous? Can you think of the advantages/benefits of space exploration? Do you remember the first landing on the moon? Would you go to the moon if you had the chance?

Getting the Main Idea

A. Listen to the conversation. Listen for the main ideas only.

B. Discuss your answers to the preview questions. Were your predictions correct? How do Linda and Jeff feel about space travel and exploration? How does Gloria feel?

95

Stress

C. Listen to the conversation again and fill in the missing stressed words.

    Jeff: Gloria! Linda! Come _____ to the

                _____ ! You've _____

                _____ see this _____ !

  Linda: Look how _____ and _____ it is!

  Gloria: It _____ as if you could _____

                _____ and _____ it.

    Jeff: Remember, in _____ , when Neil Armstrong

                _____ on the moon? Just think—his_____

            are still there.

  Gloria: Really?

    Jeff: Sure. There's no _____ on the moon—

                _____ to _____ them

                _____ .

  Gloria: Hm, that's _____ , but I _____

            understand why so much _____ is spent on

                _____ exploration when we have _____

            many _____ right here on _____ .

  Linda: Actually, the _____ of money that's

                _____ on the _____

                _____ is relatively _____

            compared to what we _____ on

                _____ programs. And _____ ,

            you have to _____ the _____ and

                _____ benefits of space exploration.

  Gloria: Like _____ ?

    Jeff: Well, for example, _____ are used for

                _____ _____ and for locating

                _____ deposits. This helps the

                _____ countries like _____

as well as the _____ nations like the _____

_____ .

D. Now listen to the first part of the conversation again. Repeat each sentence after the speaker. Remember: stressed words are *louder and clearer* than unstressed words.

E. Listen to the rest of the conversation and write the important (stressed) words. Your notes should look like a telegram.

Linda: _____

_____

_____

_____

_____

Jeff: _____

_____

Astronaut Neil Armstrong took this picture of crew member Edwin Aldrin during their historic walk on the moon.

Gloria: _____

_____

Jeff: _____

_____

Gloria: _____

_____

Linda: _____

_____

_____

_____

_____

_____

_____

Gloria: _____

Jeff: _____

_____

_____

Gloria: _____

_____

F. Using your notes, reconstruct the conversation with a partner, orally or in writing.

PART II. LECTURE

Context: The following talk is about the possible effect of the moon on our behavior.

Preview questions: What are some of the beliefs about the full moon and its effects in your culture? How does the moon affect our physical environment?

Vocabulary: The following terms appear in the lecture. Try to understand them from the context they are in; do not use a dictionary. After the lecture, you will be asked to write a brief definition of each term.

worship	tide	linked to
mystery	phase	commit suicide

diameter   unpredictable   associated with
gravity   heiress   oddly
                                                   erratic

A. Listen to the lecture. Follow the outline as you listen. Do not write anything at this point.

B. Listen again and fill in the outline.

OUTLINE
The Effects of the Moon

I. Introduction: Facts about the moon

   A. Distance from earth: _____

   B. Diameter: _____

   C. Gravity: _____

   D. The moon affects:

      1. _____

   2. Earthquakes (possibly)

II. Moon definitely affects behavior of _____

   Example: _____

III. Does moon affect _____?

   A. Carl Sagan: _____

   B. Arnold Lieber wrote book: *The Lunar Effect*

      1. _____ _____ go up during full moon

         a. Sarah Jane Moore: _____

         b. Patricia Hearst: _____

      2. Moon linked to _____

         Example: _____

   C. L.A. police and fire department say _____

      1. Fire department says highest number of _____ occurs dur-
         ing full moon

      2. Police sergeant says most police officers think that

         _____

      3. People who deal directly with public agree:

         _____ , _____ , bartenders,

         _____ .

IV. Some people _____

   A. L.A. policeman Duane Rasure: _____

      _____

   B. Bar owner: people can be erratic at any time

V. Conclusion.

   A. For the next few months, you should _____

      _____

   B. Be glad the earth has only one moon.

      1. _____ has twenty-two.

      2. Jupiter has _____ major ones and _____
         minor ones.

C. Listen to the following questions and write the answers.

1. What do scientists know about the moon's effects on the earth?

   _____

2. How does the moon affect the behavior of animals?

   _____

   _____

3. Who believes that the full moon changes our behavior and what examples do they give?

   _____

   _____

   _____

   _____

4. Who has the opposite point of view?

   _____

   _____

   _____

D. *Vocabulary review.* Define these terms as they were used in the lecture.

1. worship: _____

   _____

2. mystery: _____

   _____

3. diameter: _____

   _____

4. gravity: _____

   _____

5. tide: _____

   _____

6. phase: _____

   _____

7. unpredictable: _____

8. heiress: _____

9. linked to: _____

10. commit suicide: _____

11. associated with: _____

12. oddly: _____

13. erratic: _____

PART III. MAKING INFERENCES

Listen to the following information about the solar system. Draw conclusions based on the facts you hear. Circle the best answer. You will hear each item twice.

1. a. requires expensive technology
   b. is ancient
   c. is a modern invention

2. a. the earth is part of the Milky Way
   b. the solar system is larger than a galaxy
   c. the sun revolves around the Milky Way

3. a. closer to the earth than to the sun
   b. closer to the sun than the earth is
   c. farther from the sun than the earth is

4. a. not all astronauts are pilots
   b. astronauts must have Ph.D.'s
   c. astronauts must study astronomy in college

5. a. three meters
   b. twelve meters
   c. one-half meter

PART IV. LISTENING TASK

Look at the map of the solar system. Familiarize yourself with the information you see. Can you name some of the planets? Now listen to the descriptions of the different bodies that make up our solar system. As you listen, write the names of the bodies in the correct places on the map. Refer to the list below for spelling.

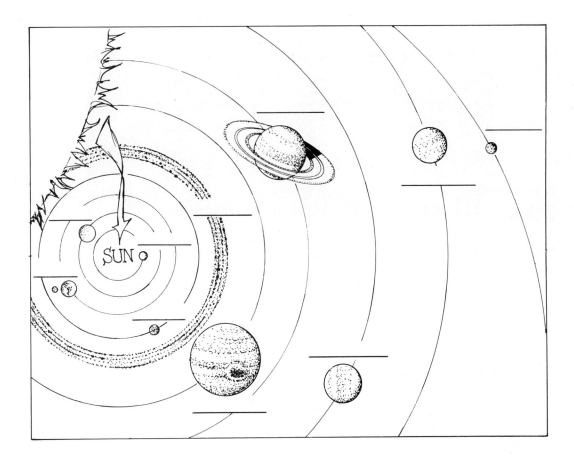

asteroids	Mercury	Uranus
earth	Neptune	Venus
Jupiter	Pluto	sun
Mars	Saturn	

PART V. SPEAKING ACTIVITIES

A. *Role-play.* Act out the following situations in groups of two or three.

1. You're applying for a job as an astronaut. A NASA panel interviews you. To prepare for the interview, listen again to the qualifications on the tape for Part III, Question 4.

2. Several extraterrestrials have just landed in a flying saucer behind your school. Interview them. Find out where they're from, how long they have been traveling, how their craft operates, how they differ from earthlings, etc.

B. *Activity.* Imagine you are a member of a space crew. Your spaceship has crash-landed on the lighted side of the moon. Another spaceship will pick you up about two hundred miles away. Since you will have to walk there, you can take only a limited number of items with you. Below are fifteen items your crew will have to choose from. Read the items and use your dictionary if necessary to understand their meanings. Then decide which items are the *most important* and which are the least important. Place the number 1 by the most important item, the number 2 by the second most important, and so on.* Compare your rankings with those of your neighbors.

_____ box of matches   *telescope*   *light source*

_____ dried food   *comb/brush*   *a mirror*

                         soap   *knife*

                         antiseptic   *cigarette*

*Based on Jay Hall's "NASA Exercise" in Psychology Today, *1971, 5(6), pp. 51–54, 86, 88.*

_____ fifty feet of nylon rope

_____ parachute silk

_____ portable heating unit

_____ two pistols

_____ one case of dehydrated milk

_____ two one-hundred pound tanks of oxygen

_____ map of the moon's constellations

_____ life raft

_____ magnetic compass

_____ five gallons of water

_____ first-aid kit containing injection needles

_____ solar-powered FM receiver-transmitter

C. *Discussion.*

1. In Part I, Jeff and Linda talk about the benefits of space exploration. Give other examples to support their argument that space exploration has benefited all of us.

2. Do you believe that life exists on other planets?

3. Do you believe in UFOs (*unidentified flying objects*, like "flying saucers")?

4. Do you believe that a full moon makes people behave strangely?

10

MEDICINE, MYTHS, AND MAGIC

PART I. PHONOLOGICAL CLUES

Context: Linda and Gloria come home from school and find Jeff in bed watching television. It's the middle of the afternoon.

Preview questions: Why is Jeff probably at home watching t.v.? How will Gloria and Linda react? What will they recommend?

Getting the Main Idea

A. Listen to the conversation. Listen for the main ideas only.

B. Discuss your answers to the preview questions. Were your predictions correct? What's wrong with Jeff? What cures do Linda and Gloria know for the flu?

Stress

C. Listen to the conversation again and fill in the missing stressed words.

Linda: _____ ?

Gloria: _____ _____ ?

Linda: Jeff, _____ are you at

_____ at _____ in the

_____ ?

Jeff: I've got the _____ . My _____ aches,

I've got a _____ of _____ , my

_____ won't stop _____ ,

everything hurts. I feel like I'm going to _____ .

Linda: Don't be _____ , you're _____ going

to _____ . I'll go _____ you some of

Grandma's _____ soup. Meanwhile, let's get some

_____ in this _____ ; it's

_____ _____ in here.

Gloria: _____ ! My _____ always said you

should _____ when you have the

_____ to reduce the _____ .

Maybe you _____ open the _____ .

Linda: Oh, that's an _____ _____ ,

_____ .

D. Now listen to the first part of the conversation again. Repeat each sentence after the speaker. Remember: stressed words are *louder and clearer* than unstressed words.

E. Listen to the rest of the conversation and write the important (stressed) words. Your notes should look like a telegram.

Gloria: _____

Linda: _____

_____

_____

Jeff: _____

Linda: _____

Gloria: _____

_____

_____

Linda: _____

_____

_____

_____

_____

Jeff: _____

_____

T.V.: _____

_____

_____

Jeff: _____

_____

F. Using your notes, reconstruct the conversation with a partner, orally or in writing.

PART II. LECTURE

Context: The following lecture is about an area in the Atlantic Ocean where many mysterious things have happened over the years.

Preview questions: Has anything mysterious ever happened to you? What do you know about the Bermuda Triangle? Can you think of any other natural phenomenon that is in some way mysterious or unexplained?

Vocabulary: The following terms appear in the lecture. Try to understand them from the context they are in; do not use a dictionary. After the lecture, you will be asked to write a brief definition of each term.

compass	canyons
search	magnetic
wreckage	navigator
survivors	theory
features	creature
current	

A. Listen to the lecture. Follow the outline as you listen. Do not write anything at this point.

B. Listen again and fill in the outline.

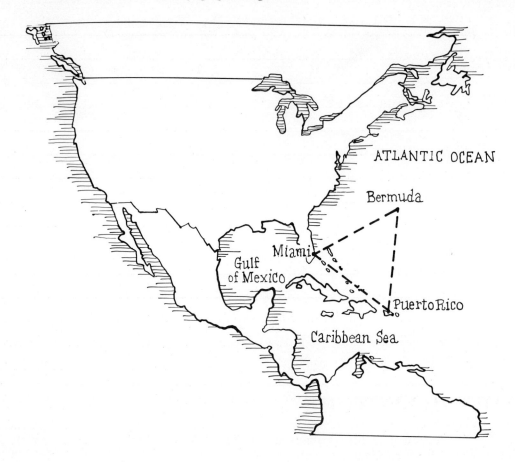

OUTLINE

The Bermuda Triangle

I. Introduction

Story about: _____

_____

II. Facts about the Triangle

A. Location: _____

B. Disappearances: _____

_____

C. Rest of lecture will be about: _____

_____

III. _____

    A. Accidents are the result of _____ .

       These include:

       1. Gulf Stream current

       2. _____

       3. _____

       4. _____

    B. Conclusion: _____

       _____

IV. Other theories

    A. John Wallace Spencer: _____

       _____

    B. _____

V. Conclusion: _____

    _____

C. Listen to the following questions and write the answers.

    1. Where is the Bermuda Triangle? _____

       _____

    2. What is mysterious about it? _____

       _____

    3. What is the U.S. Navy's explanation of the mystery?

       _____

       _____

       _____

    4. What are some other theories concerning the mystery?

       _____

       _____

       _____

    5. Which theory do you believe? _____

       _____

D. *Vocabulary review.* Define these terms as they were used in the lecture.

1. compass: _____

_____

2. search: _____

_____

3. wreckage: _____

_____

4. survivors: _____

_____

5. features: _____

_____

6. current: _____

_____

7. canyons: _____

_____

8. magnetic: _____

_____

9. navigator: _____

_____

10. theory: _____

_____

11. creature: _____

_____

PART III. MAKING INFERENCES

Listen to the following conversations. Decide who the speakers are. Circle the best answer. You will hear each item twice.

1. a. an astrologer
 b. a linguist
 c. a fortuneteller

2. a. a doctor
b. a tooth fairy
c. the child's mother

3. a. a doctor
b. someone's grandfather
c. a fortuneteller

4. a. a doctor
b. a waiter
c. a neighbor

5. a. a history teacher
b. a psychiatrist
c. an astrologer

PART IV. LISTENING TASK

Look at the drawing of the neck and the abdominal cavity. Can you name some of the organs? Look at the list below. Pronounce each word after the speaker. Then listen to the descriptions of different organs and write their names in the correct places in the drawing on the next page.

intestine	pancreas
appendix	thyroid
diaphragm	larynx
liver	aorta
lungs	bladder
gallbladder	

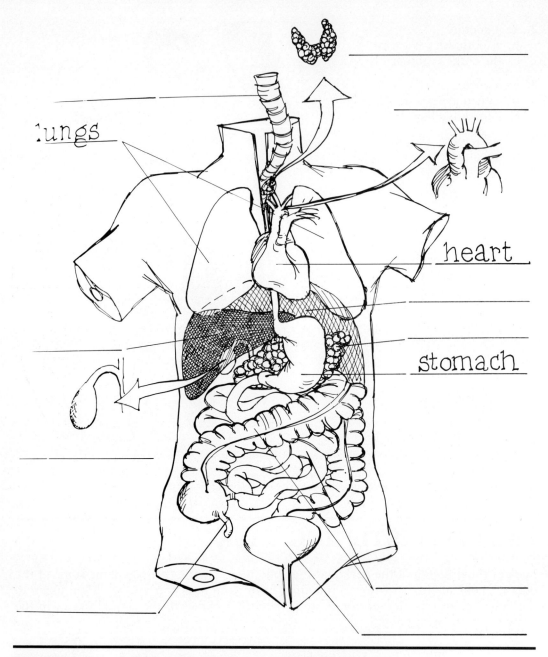

lungs

heart

stomach

PART V. SPEAKING ACTIVITIES

A. *Discussion.*

1. What's your astrological sign? Do you believe in astrology? Do you take astrological advice seriously?

2. Are you superstitious? What superstitions does your culture have about: food, marriage, luck, animals, the weather, numbers, colors, health, etc.? Here are some examples of superstitions common in the United States and Canada. Do you have the same or similar superstitions in your culture?

Finding a four-leaf clover brings good luck.

A rabbit's foot is good luck.
If you see a falling star, you can make three wishes and they will come true.

Walking under a ladder or seeing a black cat cross your path is bad luck.
The number 13 is bad luck.
When your nose itches, it means that company is coming.

3. Do you believe in the following things? Why or why not? Do most people in your culture feel the same way you do?

- ghosts and other spirits
- the "evil eye" (that someone can cause others to have bad luck through magical powers—or just by looking at them in a certain way)
- extrasensory perception (ESP: the ability to know things beyond what your

five senses tell you, to make predictions about something you couldn't know under normal circumstances—the death of someone, for instance)
- the devil

B. *Activities.*

1. In groups, look at the following list of physical ailments. Choose one and interview each member of the group about a treatment. Are the treatments folk remedies, "old wives' tales," or medical treatments?

cold	stomach ache	burn
rheumatism	baldness	eye infection
hiccups	warts	bad breath
cough	dry skin	high blood pressure
sore throat	toothache	

2. Read your astrological forecast in the newpaper for three days. Report to the class about its accuracy and appropriateness.

C. *Role-play.*

1. With a partner, act out a conversation between a fortuneteller and his or her client. The client is interested in:

- his or her love life
- financial situation
- career
- health
- whether he or she will have children

   Example: "Will I meet someone and fall in love soon?"

2. Work in groups: A group of doctors appears at a press conference and announces an important medical discovery. Decide what kind of discovery it will be and play the roles of the doctors and reporters; the reporters want to know how the discovery was made, what purposes it will accomplish, how much it will cost, and so forth.

11
THE MEDIA

PART I. PHONOLOGICAL CLUES

Context: Gloria and Dan have just returned from seeing a film. Gloria is upset about the movie.

   Preview questions: What type of movie might they have seen? What kind of film do *you* find upsetting?

Getting the Main Idea

A. Listen to the conversation. Listen for the main ideas only.

B. Discuss your answers to the preview questions. Did you predict why Gloria was upset about the movie? What was Dan's point of view?

Stress

C. Listen to the conversation again and fill in the missing stressed words.

    Jeff: Gloria, what's _____ ? _____ you

                _____ the movie?

    Gloria: No, I _____ . I don't see the _____ of

              such _____ movies. And I don't think they should be

              _____ .

    Dan: _____ a minute. You _____ how full

              the _____ was. _____ a lot of people

              _____ to see movies like that. And you have

              _____ _____ to tell them that they

              _____ .

              People who _____ it's _____ can

              _____ _____ .

    Gloria: But I _____ know it was going to be so

              _____ .

    Dan: Come _____ , Gloria, _____ is

              violent! Movies are _____ to be a

              _____ of _____ life.

D. Now listen to the first part of the conversation again. Repeat each sentence after the speaker. Remember: stressed words are *louder and clearer* than unstressed words.

E. Listen to the rest of the conversation and write the important (stressed) words. Your notes should look like a telegram.

    Jeff: _____

           _____

           _____

    Dan: _____

           _____

    Gloria: _____

           _____

    Dan: _____

_____

_____

Gloria: _____

_____

Dan: _____

_____

_____

_____

Gloria: _____

F. Using your notes, reconstruct the conversation with a partner, orally or in writing.

PART II. LECTURE

Context: The following lecture describes the various types of media used in advertising.

   Preview questions: What does *media* mean? Why are media important for advertising? What are the advantages and disadvantages of various media for advertisers (for example, newspapers and magazines, t.v., radio, the mail, billboards)?

Television viewers see many ads on commercial stations.

Other popular advertising media include magazines, newspapers, and billboards.

Vocabulary: The following terms appear in the lecture. Try to understand them from the context they are in; do not use a dictionary. After the lecture, you will be asked to write a brief definition of each term.

persuade	ads
medium	broadcast
the media	billboards
information sources	commercial
advertisement	category

A. Listen to the lecture. Follow the outline as you listen. Do not write anything at this point.

B. Listen again and fill in the outline.

OUTLINE
Advertising and the Media

I. Introduction

    A. Advertising is important to companies because _____

_____

    B. Three categories of media:

        1. _____

        2. _____

        3. _____

II. The print media consist of _____ and _____

    A. _____

        1. Advantages

            a. _____

            b. _____

            c. _____

        2. _____

            a. No color

            b. _____

    B. Magazines

        1. One great advantage: _____

        2. Disadvantage: _____

III. _____ media: _____ and

    _____ .

    A. Radio

        1. Advantages

            a. _____

            b. _____

        2. _____

            a. _____

            b. _____

    B. _____

        1. _____

            a. Sound, movement, and color—dramatic

            b. Everybody watches it

            c. Ads are seen nationally

    2. Disadvantages: _____

IV. Direct media

    A. _____

        1. Advantage: _____

        2. Disadvantage: _____

    B. Billboards

        1. Advantages:

           a. _____

           b. _____

           c. _____

        2. Disadvantage: _____

    C. Signs and posters, used in point of purchase advertising

        Example: _____

        Advantage: _____

V. Conclusion: _____

_____ .

C. Listen to the following questions and write the answers.

    1. What are the three main categories of media used in advertising? What examples belong to each category?

        _____

        _____

        _____

    2. Why do newspapers receive more advertising money than any other medium?

        _____

        _____

    3. What are the advantages and disadvantages of these media: newspapers, magazines, radio, t.v., direct mail, billboards, and signs or posters?

        _____

        _____

_____

_____

_____

_____

_____

4. How does an advertiser decide where to place his ad?

_____

_____

_____

D. *Vocabulary review.* Define these terms as they were used in the lecture.

1. persuade: _____

_____

2. medium: _____

_____

3. the media: _____

_____

4. information sources: _____

_____

5. advertisement: _____

_____

6. ads: _____

_____

7. broadcast: _____

_____

8. billboards: _____

_____

9. commercial: _____

_____

10. category: _____

_____

PART III. MAKING INFERENCES

You will hear selections from various newspaper articles. First, familiarize yourself with the sections of the newspaper below. Then listen carefully and decide in *which section* of the newspaper the articles probably appeared. Write the letters in the blanks.

a. the travel section
b. the business section
c. the editorial/opinion page
d. the sports section
e. the classified ads
f. the front page
g. the weather section
h. the entertainment section

1. _____   5. _____

2. _____   6. _____

3. _____   7. _____

4. _____

PART IV. LISTENING TASK

Before listening to the following telephone survey, look at the questionnaire below. What do you think is the purpose of the survey?

As you listen to the conversation, take the role of the caller and fill out the form based on the information you hear.

SURVEY

I. RESPONDENT'S BIOGRAPHICAL DATA

Age: 25–35   _____   Marital status: Single   _____

     36–45   _____   Married   _____

     46–55   _____   Divorced   _____

     56 and above   _____

Occupation: _____

Yearly income: $15,000–20,000 _____

                  20,000–30,000 _____

                  30,000–40,000 _____

                  40,000–50,000 _____

                  above 50,000   _____

II. NEWSPAPERS

                                    Subscribe?

Name(s): _____   Yes _____   No _____

         _____   Yes _____   No _____

         _____   Yes _____   No _____

Hours read per week: _____

III. MAGAZINES

Subscribe?

Name(s): _____   Yes _____   No _____

_____   Yes _____   No _____

_____   Yes _____   No _____

Hours read per week: _____

IV. BOOKS

Type of books read: biographies   _____

mysteries   _____

science fiction   _____

novels   _____

self-help books   _____

textbooks   _____

other   _____

Amount of time spent reading a week: _____

Book club member: Yes _____   No _____

V. TELEVISION

Number of t.v. sets in household _____

Hours per week watched: _____

PART V. SPEAKING ACTIVITIES

A. *Role-play.* In groups of two or three, act out one of the following situations. Resolve the problem in each skit.

1. You and your wife or husband have a ten-year-old child. He has asked for permission to stay up late and watch a movie. You know that the movie contains a certain amount of violence. You don't want your child to see it. Your husband or wife disagrees.

2. You have just discovered a pornographic magazine in your thirteen-year-old son's room. You decide to speak to him about it. Decide what questions you will ask your son and whether you will punish him or not.

3. You are sixteen years old. You are trying to get into an R-rated movie, for adults, by using your friend's I.D. card. The ticket vendor is suspicious.

B. *Activities.*

1. As a class, make up a questionnaire similar to the one in Part IV about people's t.v. watching habits. Then interview three Americans and report your findings to the class.

2. Choose a product and design three ads for it: one for t.v., one for a magazine, and one for the radio. How will these ads differ?

C. *Discussion.*

1. Are there situations where censorship is useful or justifiable? If you think so, give an example.

2. Is there censorship of the media in your country? Do you agree with your government's policy on censorship? Are pornographic magazines available in your country? Do you think they should be or should not be?

3. Where do you get most of your news: radio, television, or newspapers? Do you notice a difference between newspapers here and newspapers in your country?

12
PREJUDICE, TOLERANCE, AND JUSTICE

PART I. PHONOLOGICAL CLUES

Context: Jeff is applying for a secretarial job in a doctor's office. He is being interviewed by the office manager.

Preview questions: What questions will the office manager probably ask Jeff? Is it unusual for a man to apply for a job as a secretary?

Getting the Main Idea

A. Listen to the conversation. Listen for the main ideas only.

B. Discuss your answers to the preview questions. Were your predictions correct? What questions did the office manager ask Jeff? Why didn't Jeff expect to get the job?

Stress

C. Listen to the conversation again and fill in the missing stressed words.

Manager: Mr. Evans, on your _____ , you

_____ your _____ as

"musician." You _____ say that you're a

_____ . Would you _____

telling me _____ you're applying for a

_____ in an _____ ?

Jeff: As you _____ _____ , it's pretty

_____ to make a _____ as a

_____ . _____ _____

work at _____ jobs during the

_____ .

Manager: I'm _____ that your _____ and your

_____ _____ may

_____ with your _____ in the

_____ .

Jeff: Well, it's _____ that I work at _____

a lot, but the _____ is _____ in the

_____ . And my _____ are in

the _____ . I don't _____

there will be any _____ .

Manager: Let's _____ about your _____ . I

_____ that you've worked in a _____

_____ before. _____ were your

_____ ?

Jeff: I had to _____ the _____ , handle

_____ , _____ letters, and take

_____ of _____ the

_____ .

Manager: I see. _____ , Mr. Evans, you're _____

_____ for the job, but I'm _____

about the _____ that if you _____ it,

you'd be the _____ _____ working in

an _____ full of _____ . How do you

_____ about that?

Jeff: I _____ with two women, my _____

and _____ of her _____ . I don't

_____ I'd have _____

_____ .

Manager: Thank you, Mr. Evans. You'll be _____ from us.

Jeff: Thank you for your _____ .

D. Now listen to the first part of the conversation again. Repeat each sentence after the speaker. Remember: stressed words are *louder and clearer* than unstressed words.

E. Listen to the rest of the conversation and write the important (stressed) words. Your notes should look like a telegram.

Linda: _____

Jeff: _____

_____

Linda: _____

Jeff: _____

_____

_____

Linda: _____

_____

_____

Jeff: _____

The telephone rings.

Jeff: _____

Manager: _____

Jeff: _____

Manager: _____

_____

Jeff: _____

Manager: _____

Jeff: _____

Manager: _____

Jeff: _____

Linda: _____

F. Using your notes, reconstruct the conversation with a partner, orally or in writing.

Reductions

G. Listen to these examples of long and short forms from the conversation and repeat them after the speaker.

If I'd been a woman, I might have gotten it.

You should have seen her face.

H. Now listen to the following reductions. Write the *long* forms below.

1. You _____ _____ _____ that.

2. The job _____ _____ _____ taken.

3. We _____ _____ _____ if they'd asked us.

4. I _____ _____ _____ better on the test.

5. Someone _____ _____ _____ them.

PART II. LECTURE

Context: The following lecture is about an often-debated issue: prayer in public schools.

Preview questions: Do you know if children in U.S. public schools pray in class? What is the largest religious group in the United States? Which law guarantees freedom of religion in the United States? Why might prayer in public schools be a *controversial* issue?

Vocabulary: The following terms appear in the lecture. Try to understand them from the context they are in; do not use a dictionary. After the lecture, you will be asked to write a brief definition of each term.

pray	religious	prohibit
prayer	Constitution	ancestors

Above: children praying in school in the 1950s in the south of the United States.

Right: in a 1962 news conference, President John F. Kennedy says that the Supreme Court decision banning prayer in public schools gives American families an opportunity to do more praying with their children at home.

required	interpretation	amendment
religion	forbid	legal
		controversy

A. Listen to the lecture. Follow the outline as you listen. Do not write anything at this point.

B. Listen again and fill in the outline.

OUTLINE

Prayer in the U.S. Public Schools

I. Introduction

   A. Students in many parts of the United States used to _____

   _____

   B. However, _____

   _____

   C. _____

   _____

II. Two parts of the law

   A. _____

     _____

   B. _____

     _____

III. Interpretation of the law

   A. _____

     _____

   B. _____

     _____

   C. _____

     _____

   D. _____

     _____

IV. Conclusion: _____

   _____

C. Listen to the following questions and write the answers.

1. Why did some people oppose public school prayers?

   _____

   _____

   _____

2. What did the U.S. Supreme Court decide in 1962?

   _____

   _____

3. What does the Constitution say about the separation of state and religion?

   _____

   _____

   _____

4. What do supporters of public school prayer want?

_____

_____

_____

D. *Vocabulary review.* Define these terms as they were used in the lecture.

1. pray: _____

_____

2. prayer: _____

_____

3. required: _____

_____

4. religion: _____

_____

5. religious: _____

_____

6. Constitution: _____

_____

7. interpretation: _____

_____

8. forbid: _____

_____

9. prohibit: _____

_____

10. ancestors: _____

_____

11. amendment: _____

_____

12. legal: _____

_____

13. controversy: _____

_____

PART III. MAKING INFERENCES

Listen to the following information about minorities, women, and the elderly. Draw conclusions based on the facts you hear. Circle the best answer.

1. a. some jobs were open only to men
   b. some jobs were open only to women
   c. women and men often had the same job

2. a. were excellent farmers
   b. were not happy about moving to the reservations
   c. continued to make their living by hunting

3. a. life was better for black people in the North
   b. discrimination against blacks occurred in the North as well as the South
   c. black people moved north because of better job opportunities

4. a. men and women can have exactly the same jobs
   b. there are not enough doctors
   c. some jobs are still regarded as "women's work"

5. a. many older people are still capable of being creative and productive
   b. great artists always live long lives
   c. many artists do not become famous until they are old

PART IV. LISTENING TASKS

Below are three incomplete graphs. In each case, the numbers on the left represent percentages. Based on the statistics you hear, plot a bar graph for each minority group represented at the bottom.

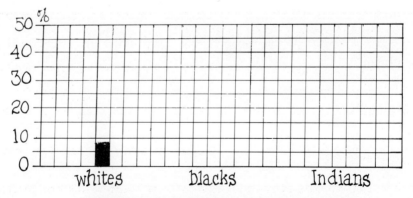

UNEMPLOYMENT RATE IN THE WORKFORCE

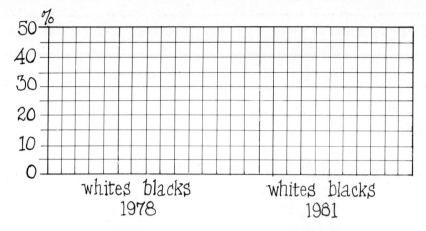

FAMILIES BELOW THE POVERTY LEVEL

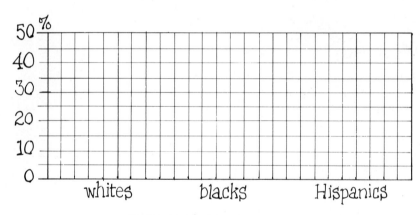

EDUCATIONAL ATTAINMENT (1982)
Males, 25 and over

PART V. SPEAKING ACTIVITIES

A. *Role-play.* Three people decide to go to court because they *think* they were discriminated against:

1. a single mother who was refused an apartment because of her two young children,

2. a fifty-one year old bank manager who was fired from his job because of his age, and

3. a black waiter who didn't get a job in a fancy restaurant in a primarily white neighborhood.

Divide your class into a jury, a judge, the three people mentioned above, and three defendants. Present the evidence and wait for the jury's decision.

B. *Activity.* In Part I, if Jeff had not gotten the job, what could he have done? Could he have hired a lawyer? Should he have? What about discrimination in housing? Do you know what people can do about it? Find out what government agency handles complaints about discrimination in housing in your town (for example, the Fair Housing Commission). Call them and find out what the procedures are in filing a complaint. Report your findings to your class.

C. *Discussion.*

1. Look at the three graphs in Part IV. What do these statistics tell us about the life of minorities as compared to whites in the United States? How might past prejudices and discrimination have caused these inequalities?

2. Is there racial prejudice in your country? Is the government doing anything about it? If so, what?

3. Do you believe in complete separation of church and state, or should the government actively support the religion of the majority? Is prayer in public schools permitted or practiced in your country?